VISITOR'S LONDON

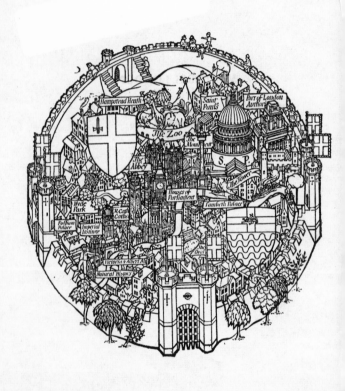

VISITOR'S
LONDON

An alphabetical

reference book for the visitor

to London by

HAROLD F. HUTCHISON

Published by

LONDON TRANSPORT

55 Broadway Westminster

London SW1

© 1954 by Harold F. Hutchison

First published 1954
2nd Edition 1955
3rd Edition 1956
4th Edition 1957
5th Edition 1958 (Revised and Enlarged)
6th Edition 1959
7th Edition 1960
8th Edition 1962
9th Edition 1963
10th Edition 1964
11th Edition 1965 (Revised and Enlarged)
12th Edition 1966
13th Edition 1967
14th Edition 1968
15th Edition 1969
16th Edition 1970
17th Edition 1971 (new cover design)
18th Edition 1972
19th Edition (Enlarged)

The illustrations in the text are by
Gareth Adamson, 7, 15, 24, 45, 56, 58, 67, 77, 90, 95, 97,
103, 104, 110, 111; William Fenton, 5, 10, 50, 52, 70,
71, 83, 84, 89, 93, 99, 105, 106, 115, 116, 120, 121;
MacDonald Gill, frontispiece; Peter Roberson, 2, 12, 18,
22, 25, 28, 31, 32, 33, 37, 46, 48, 57, 61, 65, 66, 73, 76,
80, 87, 117, 124; Ray Tooby, vi, 118; R. Wilkinson, 125;
Althea Willoughby, 39

ISBN 0 85329 032 6

Made and printed in England by Staples Printers Limited
at the Stanhope Press, Rochester, Kent

THIS ALPHABETICAL GUIDE BOOK does not pretend to be comprehensive—it is intended for the average visitor (and the inquiring Londoner) who needs a Ready Reference to London's chief buildings and places of interest.

Legend and tradition have both been eschewed in favour of matters of established fact, and the author has not hesitated to select samples for easy inspection rather than to bore the reader and weary the visitor with detailed inventories.

To have confined this guide book to London proper would have inveigled its author into many controversial decisions. He has preferred to include most places which in his opinion are worthy of note in London itself, and also some of those places in London's countryside, easily reached by the Underground, which the visitor who may tire of pavements will find both restful and refreshing.

'How to Get There' covers almost every point of interest mentioned in the text as well as many that are not. London Transport tries to keep both 'Visitor's London' and 'How to Get There' as accurate as possible (without claiming to be infallible), but redevelopment and street-widening, particularly in the City and in Dockland, mean that the scene changes almost from day to day.

Remember to ask at any London Transport ticket office or Enquiry Office for free maps of the Underground and bus services.

Admiralty Arch spans the entrance to The Mall from Trafalgar Square. It was designed by Sir Aston Webb and erected as part of the national memorial to Queen Victoria in 1910. Its triple arches can be closed by enormous wrought-iron gates.

Airports & Air Terminals. Air passengers have three points of departure by road and one by rail from the city and two airports at which to embark on their planes. B.O.A.C. headquarters are in Buckingham Palace Road near Victoria Station, B.E.A. and some of the Continental lines have headquarters at West London Air Terminal, Cromwell Road, Kensington, and Aer Lingus are at 249 Brompton Road. The British Caledonian terminal, providing a direct rail link with Gatwick Airport, is at Victoria Station.

Albany. Albany Chambers are in a Georgian mansion on the north side of Piccadilly originally built for the first Lord Melbourne by Sir William Chambers in 1770. The second son of George III was the Duke of York and Albany (p. 29) and he lived in the mansion from 1791 to 1802—hence its present name. In 1802 the mansion was sold to one Alexander Copland who decided on the novel idea of converting the house into 'residential chambers for bachelor gentlemen'. Since that revolutionary decision the Chambers have been the home of many famous men including Byron, Macaulay, Gladstone and Pinero.

Albert Hall, in Kensington Gore, was originally inspired by Prince Albert, the consort of Queen Victoria, and named after him as the 'Royal Albert Hall of Arts and Sciences'. The elliptical domed building was designed by Captain Fowke and General Scott and finished in 1871. The capacity of the hall is about 8,000, and the Victorians considered it a building 'worthy of Rome in its palmiest days'—a verdict not endorsed by succeeding generations. Efforts have been made to improve the infamous acoustics, but its exterior is a sad reflection on mid-Victorian taste. Its size, however, justifies its use for such popular musical events as the Promenade Concerts and performances by the Royal Choral Society and others. At the rear is the little-known monument to the Great Exhibition of 1851 designed in 1863 with an indifferent statue of the Prince Consort by Joseph Durham.

Albert Memorial was erected opposite the Albert Hall in Kensington Gardens to commemorate Prince Albert. It was designed by Sir George Gilbert Scott and unveiled by Queen Victoria in 1876. The statue of the Prince sitting beneath an ornate canopy holds not a bible but a catalogue of the Great Exhibition of 1851, and the surrounding groups of statuary are a good guide to the social and economic ideals of the mid-Victorian era. The whole composition is a witness to the taste of the period.

Aldgate Pump is a modern mains-water drinking fountain on the site of a pump erected over the old St. Michael's Well which had been famed in the City of London since the fifteenth century.

Alexandra Palace, on Muswell Hill, was first built in 1873. It was rebuilt to its present design only two years later after a devastating fire. The Great Hall seats 7,000 people and had one of the finest concert organs in Europe. The Palace's unprepossessing bulk dominates the surrounding area and the terrace offers commanding views far over London and the Home Counties. The grounds are popular and the amenities include a roller-skating rink, an artificial ski-slope and a boating lake. The Palace was an early home of B.B.C. Television, and it was from here in 1936 that the world's first regular television programmes were transmitted. The studios are now used by the Open University.

All Hallows by-the-Tower is a pre-Great Fire church of both intrinsic and international interest. A Saxon doorway and cross proclaim its antiquity, its tower (the steeple is a recent addition) is the only example of Cromwellian church building in the City, and the font cover is by Grinling Gibbons. The church is the head-quarters of the Toc H Fellowship founded by its former vicar the Rev. P. B. Clayton in Flanders during the First World War, and the Toc H Parent Lamp of Maintenance burns in the sanctuary. In the crypt is a museum. William Penn was baptized in the church in 1644, and John Quincy Adams, sixth president of the U.S.A., was married here.

All Souls' Church, Langham Place, was built to the design of John Nash in 1822–4. Its simple slender spire was designed as the 'vertical feature' punctuating the stucco arcades of the old Regent Street, but the ugly cliffs of the B.B.C. buildings have ruined Nash's brilliant vista. The church's interesting galleried Georgian interior has been restored to its pre-war beauty.

Auction Rooms in London are many and fascinating. The two most famous are CHRISTIE'S, founded in 1766 at 8 King Street off St. James's Street, and SOTHEBY'S (1744) at 34 New Bond Street. Christie's specialize in works of art, and Sotheby's in works of art, rare books and manuscripts. Auctions are advertised in the *Daily Telegraph* on Mondays and *The Times* on Tuesdays.

Australia House, at the east end of the Strand, is the headquarters of the Australian Government in London and the offices of its High Commissioner. It was opened in 1918 and its architect was A. Marshall Mackenzie. It is an imposing building but without any claims to originality or inspiration. All the interior and much of the timber and marble were brought from Australia. There is a reference library as well as reading and writing rooms.

B

Bank of England, in Threadneedle Street, was incorporated by Royal Charter in 1694 to finance the French wars —it has since become the cornerstone of British governmental finance. It is the banker of the Government on whose behalf it manages the note issue. In 1946 it was brought under public control. The old Bank built by Sir John Soane in the late eighteenth and early nineteenth centuries was drastically redesigned by Sir Herbert Baker between 1925 and 1939. Sir Herbert retained Soane's outer wall and Corinthian columns, and contained a new seven-storey building within these walls with sculptures by Sir Charles Wheeler above the portico. The vaults hold the nation's gold reserve. In 1780 the Bank was threatened by the Gordon 'No Popery' rioters, and since that date a military night-guard has been posted. The gowns of scarlet and gold worn on occasion by the Bank's Gate-Keepers are a welcome splash of colour in the City. They are a reminder too— with the pink coats and scarlet waistcoats of the Bank Messengers—of the early days of 'The Old Lady of Threadneedle Street', for the uniforms date from the Bank's foundation and are modelled on the livery of the servants of the first Governor.

Banqueting House, in Whitehall, is the Banqueting House of the old Whitehall Palace. It was designed by Inigo Jones and completed in 1622. It watched Charles I walk

through to his scaffold
at the north-west corner,
it heard Parliament ask
Cromwell to 'magnify
himself with the title of
King', and it listened
with Charles II to an
address of loyalty from
Parliament at the Restor-
ation. The great painted
ceiling earned Flemish
Rubens his English

knighthood and £3,000 from Charles I. The interior,
cleared of the martial miscellany which long disfigured
it, is now restored to something like its original splen-
dour, and can be visited when the building is not in use
for official functions.

Battersea Park was laid out in 1856–7 by dumping soil
excavated from the Royal Victoria Dock into what was
then unreclaimed swamp. It is today a beautiful park
with a fine river frontage, excellent playing fields, a
picturesque boating lake and a pretty old-English
garden. There is a small herd of deer and a children's zoo
with both familiar and unfamiliar pets. The lighter side of
London's contribution to the 1951 Festival of Britain
was staged in the riverside portion of the Park (p. 33),
and still survives.

H.M.S. Belfast is a recent newcomer to London's
tourist roundabout. It is the largest and most powerful
cruiser ever built for the Royal Navy, and, as the last
surviving big-gun ship, it has been presented to a special
Trust as a permanent Royal Navy museum. Moored on
the south bank of the Thames opposite the Tower, it
is an appropriate and impressive addition to the Pool
of London.

Berkeley Square in Mayfair was first laid out in 1698 and some Georgian residences still remain. On the west side is No. 45, where lived Lord Clive. There are some magnificent plane trees in the gardens planted in the mid-eighteenth century, and the shelter in the centre is late Georgian. Nightingales are possible but rare.

Bethnal Green Museum is itself a museum piece—a very important surviving example of the iron and glass construction made famous by Paxton's Crystal Palace at the Great Exhibition of 1851. The roof is the original designed by Sir William Cubitt for the South Kensington Museum. It is now enclosed in brick. The museum is a branch of the Victoria and Albert Museum and was first opened in 1872. It contains a superb collection of dolls' houses mostly of the Georgian and Victorian periods, a fine collection of period dresses, and many examples of the craftsmanship of the local Spitalfields silk industry. Among the paintings is Turner's 'St. Michael's Mount, Cornwall', and there is an excellent collection of English silver. The Keeper's house in the grounds is good early Georgian.

Billingsgate. The site of this famous fish market has been a port and quay from very early times, and the 'gate' was probably one of the two river gates in the wall of the Roman city, the other being Dowgate. It is about 200 yards down river from London Bridge. Until the beginning of the eighteenth century Billingsgate was not primarily a market for fish but for coal and corn. A statute of 1699 established it as a free fish market, and between 1848 and 1874 it was rebuilt and enlarged. These alterations destroyed its character as a haunt of bargees and vituperative women which had made the name of Billingsgate a byword for foul language before the time of Shakespeare. Some fish porters still wear an interesting flat headgear originally known as a 'bobbing hat'. 'Bobbing' is the charge made by porters to carry fish from the wholesaler to the retailer. Today the hats are referred to as 'leather hats' and are made of wood and leather. They enable a skilful porter to carry on his head about a hundredweight of fish—many are handed down from father to son and have been in the market for years.

Blackheath was the wild heathland which gave ample scope to eighteenth-century highwaymen. It is now a fine open space with the beautiful eighteenth-century houses

of the crescent known as The Paragon on its south-east corner, and nearby the lovely seventeenth-century Morden College (p. 70).

Bloomsbury Squares. London has never been thoroughly 'planned'—it has just grown. From the late seventeenth century to the early nineteenth, however, serious efforts were sometimes made to replace mediaeval chaos by civic order, and the Bloomsbury squares were a splendid fruit of this progressive movement. They were planned to provide town houses for landed gentry and homes for wealthy city business men on the principle of terraced houses surrounding piazzas. The piazzas became tree-shaded gardens. These garden-oases still stud Bloomsbury—if sometimes traffic-beset and not always open to stroll in. Go to Bedford Square to see the garden still wholly framed in the grace, elegance and dignity of Georgian urban architecture. Take a glimpse at Bedford Place which is still as its Georgian architect left it. At least you can walk through the garden of ravaged Russell Square, and there are still traces of an age of reason and proportion in Bloomsbury Square, Tavistock Square, Tavistock Place and Mecklenburgh Square.

Boat Race is the annual race from Putney to Mortlake which takes place in late March or early April between rowing eights representing the universities of Oxford and Cambridge. It provides spectators with a few minutes' free thrill and sixteen oarsmen with twenty minutes' expensive agony. The race was first rowed at Henley in 1829, but since 1856 it has been an annual event on the London Thames.

Bond Street is strictly New Bond Street at its Oxford Street end and Old Bond Street at its Piccadilly end, and takes its name from the Sir Thomas Bond who first planned it as long ago as 1686. In this fashionable 'high street of Mayfair' the display of elegant clothes and jewellery is on both sides of the shop windows, and in or near it are many of the private dealers' galleries whose changing exhibitions (mostly free) of old and modern art supplement the permanent displays of London's public galleries. At the corner of New Bond Street and Bruton Street is the Time and Life Building, completed in 1952. It is a summing-up, regardless of dollar expense, of the then current trends in interior décor and includes as a balustrade some of the abstract carving of Henry Moore.

Bridges. Between the sea and Teddington (where the first lock keeps back the tide) the Thames is crossed by 18 road and 9 railway bridges. Not all are of any great interest or merit but the following are noteworthy:

   Albert Bridge, opened in 1873, is an interesting combination of the cantilever and suspension principles— it was designed by R. M. Ordish. It is inadequate for modern road traffic and its future is uncertain.

Chelsea Bridge, opened in 1937, is an excellent example of the suspension principle—it was designed by the architects of the London County Council.

Hammersmith Bridge, opened in 1887, is a heavy and clumsy suspension bridge which incorporates the abutments and lower parts of the towers of an earlier bridge. From it there is a good view of the eighteenth-century houses of Hammersmith Mall (p. 43).

London Bridge was for centuries the only bridge across the lower Thames. In the Middle Ages it had nineteen arches carrying houses, shops and, in the middle, a chapel. The heads of the executed were placed on the spikes of the drawbridge gate. It was this bridge that was falling down in the nursery rhyme. The restriction of water by its arches caused the Thames to freeze over completely above the bridge in severe winters, and this allowed Frost Fairs to be held on the ice. Its successor was built in 1831 and its lamp-posts were cast from cannon captured during the Peninsular War. Inadequate for modern traffic, it has recently been dismantled, and re-erected in the U.S.A. The new London Bridge, built round it—without interrupting road or river traffic— gives a fine panorama of the City sky-line.

Tower Bridge is one of London's most famous landmarks. It is a masterpiece of engineering clothed in the fanciful garb of Victorian Gothic. Designed by Sir Horace Jones and Sir John Wolfe Barry, the bridge was opened in 1894—it cost more than a million pounds. The hydraulic machinery, which lifts the bascules to permit the passage of large ships, has never failed. It is called on very rarely indeed now that cargo vessels dock farther down river, but lucky visitors may still see it in action.

Waterloo Bridge was designed by Sir Giles Gilbert Scott and the engineers of the L.C.C.—it is the most beautiful of London's bridges. It is of steel and concrete and was completed in 1939. Its five graceful shallow arches are each about 240 feet wide, and the roadway permits six lanes of traffic. It worthily replaced the famous bridge of John Rennie which had developed serious weaknesses and was much too narrow for modern transport.

Westminster Bridge is a graceful cast-iron bridge (1862) whose flat arches harmonize well with the neo-Gothic of the Houses of Parliament. Wordsworth's famous sonnet refers to the bridge it replaced, but the view today is just as inspiring—it commands the Houses of Parliament, the elegant Vickers skyscraper, the new St. Thomas's Hospital, and, downriver, the Victoria Embankment, County Hall and the South Bank, with the Post Office Tower and the Barbican towers as modernist backdrop. On the north corner of the western end is Thomas Thorneycroft's statue of Queen Boadicea erected in 1902.

British Museum, in Bloomsbury, was designed by the brothers Robert and Sydney Smirke and built between 1823 and 1847—it is the world's largest museum. The porticoed south front was the work of Robert, and the reading-room and dome the work of Sydney. Its library has the right to one copy of every publication printed in this country and its magnificent domed reading-room is used by scholars from all over the world. Its print room is famous. But the glory of the

Museum for the visitor who is pressed for time—and for those who find all museums a weariness—can be pleasantly sampled by seeing at least two exhibits. First, the Rosetta Stone in the Southern Egyptian Gallery whose inscriptions in Greek, in the demotic character, and Egyptian hieroglyphics first enabled scholars to read the history of Egypt. Second, the Elgin Marbles which were brought from Greece by the Earl of Elgin in 1802–4 when he was our Ambassador in Constantinople. They are sculptures from the Parthenon's frieze, the Erechtheum and other ancient Athenian buildings, and occupy their own magnificent Duveen Gallery. A very successful personal Sound Guide system is installed. And before the visitor leaves, he must spend enough time in the manuscript room to stand in awe in front of an original Magna Carta, and to read the last poignant pages of Captain Scott's Antarctic diary. The Museum of Mankind (the Ethnography Department) is temporarily but magnificently housed at Burlington Gardens.

British Piano and Musical Museum, in an unexpected neo-Gothic setting near Kew Bridge, is an endearingly informal array of working examples of the mechanical reproducers of music so popular before the days of gramophone and radio. The main importance of the *Violano-Virtuoso*, the *Hupfeld Clavitist Expression Piano* and the *Imhof and Mukle Orchestrion* is as monuments to the ingenuity of man, but the sounds they produce can be quite exhilarating. Conducted tours, which are not really suitable for small children, take an hour or so.

British Theatre Museum—*see* **Leighton House.**

Broadcasting House, in Portland Place, is the headquarters of the British Broadcasting Corporation. It was designed by Val Myers and Watson Hart and completed in 1931. The building is of ferro-concrete faced with Portland stone and is in severely functional style. The sculptured group over the main entrance representing Ariel and Prospero is one of the last works of Eric Gill. From here a minute's walk down Regent Street, turning right into Cavendish Square, brings you, on the right, to Epstein's superb bronze 'Madonna and Child' above the arch of Heythrop College.

Brompton Oratory, in Brompton Road, is correctly named 'The Church of the London Oratory of St. Philip Neri' and was built in the 1880s (the dome was added in 1896). It was Roman Catholic London's tribute to Cardinal Newman—who introduced the Congregation of the Oratory to England in 1847—and his statue was later erected in the courtyard. It has a magnificent and ornate interior in the Italian Renaissance style: the statues of the apostles between the pilasters are of Carrara marble and were for 200 years in Siena Cathedral. Brompton Oratory is a fashionable church, but it is no less famed for its music and its choral recitals.

Buckingham Palace, at the west end of The Mall, has been the permanent London residence of the sovereign since Queen Victoria. It was originally a red brick mansion built for the Duke of Buckingham in 1703. Nash remodelled it in 1825, and in 1913 Sir Aston Webb reconstructed the front facing The Mall with Portland stone. When the sovereign is in residence the Royal Standard flies at the masthead night or day, and the Palace is guarded usually by sentries of the Guards Division in full dress.   The colourful ceremony

of Changing the Guard (p. 16) takes place in the forecourt, and on the monarch's official birthday the final march-past after Trooping the Colour takes place outside the gates. Facing the courtyard is the Queen Victoria Memorial—planned by Sir Aston Webb with sculpture by Sir Thomas Brock.

Bunhill Fields Burial Ground is in City Road, Finsbury. 'Bunhill' is probably a corruption of 'Bonehill', referring to the fact that here was the repository for the bones

disinterred from the Charnel Chapel of Old St. Paul's in
1547. The site became a nonconformist cemetery in the
late seventeenth century. Wall columns facing City Road
give the names of its famous dead, including John Bunyan
(1688), Defoe (1731), Isaac Watts (1748), William Blake
(1827) and many of the prolific Wesley family. The
Society of Friends also had a burial ground here, and
George Fox the founder was buried (1690) in what is
now the small recreation ground off Roscoe Street.

Burlington Arcade runs parallel to Old Bond Street and
links Burlington Gardens with Piccadilly. It is a delightful
weatherproof Regency shopping promenade in the heart
of the West End, with its own strict beadle. Its windows
are a feast of elegance, its wares are not for purses thinly
lined.

Bush House, Aldwych, is one of the earliest examples of
American commercial architecture in London. It
was designed by Helmle, Corbett & Harrison, a New
York firm of architects, and named after Irvine T.
Bush. The huge block completes the vista of Kingsway
with its two colossal figures of 'Youth' over the portico
designed by the American Malvina Hoffman and inscribed 'To the friendship of the English-speaking
people'. It was completed in 1931.

Bushy Park. The mile-long Chestnut Avenue of Bushy
Park, Teddington, was planned by Sir Christopher Wren
to give a grand new approach to his projected north front
for Hampton Court Palace. The chestnut trees were first
planted in 1699 and there are also 10 miles of lime trees.
A large herd of deer live in the park, and the ornamental
ponds are well stocked with carp. In spring, the chestnuts
in full bloom provide a magnificent spectacle of natural
beauty enhanced by the planning of a genius.

C

Canada House is on the west side of Trafalgar Square. The original building was designed by Robert Smirke for the Union Club formed to commemorate the union of the English and Irish parliaments, but in 1925 it was remodelled by Septimus Warwick to bring together the scattered and rapidly expanding staff of the High Commissioner for Canada. Built in a sturdy Regency-Victorian tradition, the building forms a ponderous west side to Trafalgar Square, its cornices beloved of the pigeons and starlings. The ground floor is open to the public, and there is a library, a reading-room and an information room.

Canals are part of London's industrial heritage. The Grand Union Canal, with its extension the Regent's Canal, threads its way through North London, transforming roads into bridges and hills into locks. Virtually obsolete for industrial purposes, the canal has been taken over by the boating enthusiasts, whose base is Little Venice, a small basin near Paddington. From here, British Waterways operate in summer the Zoo Waterbus service to and from the Zoo (p. 124). Landlubbers can explore this curiously remote waterside world on foot from the Canal-side Walk, which runs for about a mile from Lisson Grove near Marylebone to the Zoo, and beyond.

Canonbury Tower, in Islington, is all that remains of the manor house of Canonbury—a relic of warm Tudor brick amind the cold stucco of later Islington. The fine oak staircase has been used by Elizabeth I, Raleigh, Francis Bacon, Oliver Goldsmith, and Charles Lamb—to name only a few of its distinguished visitors or tenants.

Carlyle's House, at 24 Cheyne Row, Chelsea, dates from the early eighteenth century, and in it Thomas Carlyle lived from 1834 until his death in 1881. The

house is still very much
as Carlyle knew it, and
on the top floor is the
room with double walls
and large skylight which
he installed in a vain
search for quiet and light
—his stove left him too
cold in the winter and the
skylight made him too
hot in summer. There are
many personal relics, and
the whole house is open as
a well-preserved memorial
museum to the Sage of

Chelsea. His statue is in the Embankment Gardens
opposite Cheyne Row.

Carnaby Street became overnight the Mecca of 'Swinging
London'. Lined like a souk with reverberating cavernous
boutiques, although overtaken by imitators elsewhere
it still provides a fascinating kaleidoscope of the best
(and worst) of modern fashion revolutions.

Cecil Sharp House, near Regent's Park, is the headquarters of the English Folk Dance and Song Society.
Cecil Sharp (1859–1924) was a pioneer in the collecting
and presentation of folk lore and folk arts. The main
hall boasts a huge mural (69 ft. × 20 ft.) from the exciting
and lavish brush of Ivon Hitchens.

Cenotaph is in Whitehall opposite the Home Office—it
was designed by Sir Edward Lutyens and unveiled on
Armistice Day 1920. In deference to men and women of
differing creeds and colours, it bears no religious symbols
and is a simply proportioned monument in Portland
stone decorated with the flags of the three services and
the mercantile marine. At 11 00 on Remembrance Sunday
the Cenotaph becomes the centre of the Commonwealth's
homage to its dead of two world wars, when a broadcast

service is held here attended by the sovereign, members of parliament, leaders of the Forces and other representatives of the national life.

Central Hall, Westminster, is the headquarters in this country of the Methodist Church. It was deliberately designed by Lanchester and Rickards in a non-Gothic style so as not to challenge Westminster Abbey across the road. It was first opened in 1912. The great hall has an excellent organ and seats 2,700 people and a full orchestra. In January 1946 it was the first home of the General Assembly of the United Nations.

Changing the Guard is a colourful ceremony which anyone can see, almost any day of the year, without charge or hindrance. The Queen's Life Guard, provided by the Household Cavalry (p. 51), is changed in the small courtyard of The Horse Guards in Whitehall. The Queen's Guard, provided by the Guards Division (p. 40), changes at Buckingham Palace. Both wear full dress and when the Queen is in London—proclaimed by the Royal Standard over Buckingham Palace—both carry Queen's Colours (Household Cavalry Colours, small enough to manage when mounted, are called 'Standards'). The Household Cavalry are quartered at Hyde Park Barracks, Knightsbridge, and can be seen every morning making their way to an from The Horse Guards, and the Guards leave from either Wellington or Chelsea Barracks. For short periods, when the Guards Division is away, one of the Line regiments is called upon to provide the Guard.

Charlton House, between Greenwich and Woolwich, dates from 1607 when it was built for the tutor of Henry, Prince of Wales, elder son of King James I. The house has been much altered internally but it is still in essentials a good example of Jacobean architecture.

Charterhouse, near Smithfield, has nothing to do with the housing of charters; the name is a corruption of 'Chartreuse' where the Carthusian Order was first founded. Here in 1371 was a monastery for Carthusian Monks; today it is a house of rest for aged 'brethren' who must belong to the Church of England, must be bachelors or widowers over sixty, and must have served as officers in the services or as members of the clergy or in one of the professions. The school was originally a foundation to give free education to forty poor scholars. The great public school into which this has developed is now located on the hills above Godalming in Surrey. The original buildings date mostly from the sixteenth century and the Grand Hall is a much restored example of the Elizabethan style. The chapel has an interesting monument to Thomas Sutton (1612) and parts of the old monastic buildings are preserved in Washhouse Court and Master's Court.

Chelsea Old Church, on the Chelsea Embankment, was a sad Second World War casualty, but fortunately the More Chapel, dating from 1528 and built by Sir Thomas More, survived. Two Renaissance capitals from the original Italian chancel are probably to the design of Holbein—a great friend of More—and they remain. The fully restored church is especially rich in memorials and brasses.

Chelsea Royal Hospital was founded by Charles II in 1682. Legend says that he was influenced by Nell Gwyn, but it is more likely that he was imitating Louis XIV who in 1670 had founded the Hôtel des Invalides in Paris. The buildings were begun by Wren, added to by Robert Adam from 1765 to 1792, and completed by Sir John Soane. The central Figure Court and the Chapel are wholly Wren's work at its best. The statue in the courtyard is of Charles II and may be by Grinling Gibbons. The Council Chamber in the Governor's House is a magnificent room remodelled

by Adam and hung with portraits by Van Dyck, Lely, and Kneller. The 500 pensioners—old and invalid soldiers—wear a famous uniform: a scarlet frock coat in summer and a dark blue tunic in winter. A small but interesting museum tells the 300-year story of the Hospital and its pensioners. The gardens which extend to the Embankment are the setting for the great Chelsea Flower Show, usually presented in late May.

Chenies is a small and pretty Buckinghamshire village not far from the River Chess. Its manor house with twisted chimneys, stepped gables and turreted entrance is typically Tudor. Just off the village green is the church with the interesting private chapel (1556) of the Russell family, dukes of Bedford. In the nave of the church are some good brasses in memory of the Cheynes, who were the first lords of the manor.

Chessington Zoo, in Surrey, is a commercial enterprise set in the pretty grounds of a mansion which dates from the time of Charles II. As well as a zoo there is a circus and an amusement park.

Chislehurst is a pleasant suburb in Kent, 12 miles south-east of London. There is a large common and at the south end by the church is an old cockpit. The church contains memorials to the Walsinghams, once lords of the manor. On the west side is **Camden Place,** now the golf club house but originally built by William Camden, the antiquary, who died there in 1623. Emperor Napoleon III and Empress Eugénie of France lived there after the collapse of the Second Empire. Opposite the main gate of Camden Place is The Cedars, home of William Willett, the originator of Summer Time. One mile to the south is Petts Wood, bought by public subscription as a memorial to Willett. At the bottom of the steep hill from The Cedars, by the Bickley Arms, are the **Chisle-hurst Caves.** They were carved out of the chalk in prehistoric times. During the last war in the worst air raids, 15,000 bombed-out people were sheltered here. The war-time community was well organized and the electric light and underground church remain.

Chiswick House is one of the most interesting although the smallest of London's aristocratic mansions. It was built by Lord Burlington in 1730 in the style of his architectural master Palladio, and is a model of sym-metrical planning and subtle detail. There are two floors, the plain low-ceilinged ground floor in which Burlington had private quarters and the lofty first floor to which the ornate portico is the entrance. This was his show-piece and into its decoration William Kent poured all his artistic talent. Marble fireplaces support panels by Sebastian Ricci and there are also paintings by Kneller, Lely, and Guido Reni. The ceiling of The Gallery carries nine panels doubtfully attributed to Paul Veronese. To the north of the house is the Inigo Jones Gateway designed for Beaumont House, Chelsea, in 1621 and presented to Lord Burlington in 1737. William Kent was also commissioned to lay out the grounds and some of the statues in the gardens were brought over from Hadrian's Villa at Tivoli. The visitor to Chiswick House should make a point of also seeing **Chiswick Mall**—a riverside village of excellent mid-eighteenth-century houses, **Chiswick Square,** off Burlington Lane, of late seventeenth-century houses, and **Hogarth's House** (p. 48) in Hogarth Lane.

Church House, in Dean's Yard, Westminster, was de-signed by Sir Herbert Baker and completed in 1940 as the headquarters of the Canterbury Houses of Convocation and the National Assembly of the Church of England. During the last war the Convocation Hall was used for a time by the House of Lords and the Hoare Memorial Hall by the House of Commons.

City Churches. In spite of the towering office blocks, the towers and spires of the City Churches still hold their own on the City skyline. Before the Great Fire of 1666 there were ninety-eight churches within the City walls and ten more in the City's 'liberties' just outside the walls. Today there are some forty City churches left, some unscathed, others restored or rebuilt, and one or two with towers only, left as memorials. Each is worth a visit; but to see them all is beyond the energy of the normal visitor. This guidebook recommends its readers to climb the steps to the stone gallery of St. Paul's (p. 93), or to the platform of the Monument (p. 69), and admire the Wren spires and towers which have miraculously survived the last war. The interiors of St. Magnus the Martyr at London Bridge and St. Stephen Walbrook next door to the Mansion House are excellent samples of the grace and intelligence which Wren brought to his post-Great Fire task. But it would be a mistake for anyone to ignore those pre-Fire churches whose tombs, memorials and brasses are the history of the City fathers, and whose interest and beauty is closer to the history of the Londoner than the pattern—glorious and varied as it is—imposed on it by the personal genius of Wren and his disciples. The visitor is urged not to miss St. Bartholomew the Great (p. 87) in Smithfield, St. Ethelburga's and St. Helen's in Bishopsgate, and All Hallows by-the-Tower (p. 3).

City Companies originated in the mediaeval craft-gilds and their distinctive dresses or 'liveries'. They were craft-unions enforcing rules and regulations for apprentices as well as rigid standards of quality. Each Company comprises a Court, a Livery and Freemen. The Liveries (and Courts) have the right by ancient usage of electing the City of London's Sheriffs and Lord Mayors. A few still have connections with their crafts—the Goldsmiths for example still hallmark precious metals, and the Apothecaries survive as an examining body. All the surviving companies contribute to the government of their City and to educational, social and charitable causes.

Sixteen halls survived the last war. Today there are thirty-one halls including the *Wellington* (p. 31). During the summer months some of the halls are open to the public—revealing splendid interiors, magnificent collections of plate and some fascinating manuscripts.

Clarence House was built in 1825 for that Duke of Clarence who afterwards became King William iv. It was the official London home of Queen Elizabeth ii and the Duke of Edinburgh until the Queen's accession, when it became the London home of the Queen Mother. It is an unpretentious stuccoed mansion by Nash on the west side of the buildings clustering round St. James's Palace.

Clubland. Night-clubs need no advertisement here, but the discerning London visitor should not miss that much older clubland whose main-street is Pall Mall. The west-end clubs are the closed-shops of the Establishment—in politics, in sport and in the arts—but some of their exteriors can be admired by one and all. The stucco be-fringed *Athenaeum* by Decimus Burton has dominated Waterloo Place since 1830. Next door in Pall Mall the *Travellers'* (1832) and the *Reform* (1841) illustrate the virtuosity of Sir Charles Barry—that neo-Gothic master who also loved the High Renaissance. The *Royal Automobile Club* rightly expresses Edwardian opulence at its worst whereas in St. James's Street *Brooks's* (1788) illustrates the impeccable taste of the eighteenth century, while opposite *Boodle's* and *White's* are two of the choicest buildings in London. There are, of course, other clubs in London's West End but the visitor with architectural leanings can be well content if he manages to obtain an invitation to visit the *Arts* in Dover Street— its fine entrance hall was part of the town house of the Stanleys, earls of Derby, whose curious eagle-and-body crest is woven into the ironwork of the elegant staircase.

Cleopatra's Needle has no connection with Queen Cleopatra except that it comes from her city of Heliopolis where it was one of a pair first erected nearly 3,500 years ago. It is an obelisk of pink granite, and its hieroglyphics record the praises of Thothmes III and the victories of Rameses the Great. It was presented to Great Britain by Mehemet Ali, the Viceroy of Egypt, in 1819, and was finally set up on the Victoria Embankment near Charing Cross after an adventurous sea journey, which cost six seamen their lives, in 1878. Its twin is in Central Park, New York.

College of Arms, sometimes known as the Herald's Office or College of Heralds, has been on its present site in Queen Victoria Street since 1555. The present building dates from about 1683 and was designed by Francis Sandford, Lancaster Herald of the day. Under a Royal Charter of 1484, the College is responsible to the Crown for all matters appertaining to armorial bearings and pedigrees. The College is governed by the Duke of Norfolk who, by hereditary right, is the Earl Marshal—he is assisted by three Kings of Arms, six Heralds, and four Pursuivants. A large collection of heraldic and genealogical manuscripts is housed in the library.

Commonwealth Institute, at Kensington High Street, is a magnificent building which took the place of the old Imperial Institute erected in South Kensington as a national memorial on the occasion of Queen Victoria's Golden Jubilee in 1887, with the object of promoting a better understanding of the countries and peoples of the Commonwealth and Empire. Its exhibition galleries include excellent dioramas and there is a cinema, an art gallery, an information centre and a library.

Congress House, in Great Russell Street, is the headquarters of the Trades Union Congress. It is an interesting building opened in 1958, designed by David du R.

Aberdeen and worth seeing for its ingenious lighting and for the memorial by Epstein commemorating the sacrifices of trade unionists in the world wars. Epstein's powerful group was sculptured on the site from a solid 10-ton block of Roman stone and is set off by an impressive 'backcloth' of green Carrara marble.

Corn Exchange in 1826 was an open quadrangle in Mark Lane. The repeal of the Corn Laws (1845) saw a great increase in its business and in 1880 a new Corn Exchange was built. It was destroyed in 1941 but has since been rebuilt.

County Hall, at the south end of Westminster Bridge, is the administrative headquarters and debating chamber of the Greater London Council. It was designed by Ralph Knott in an Edwardian version of the Italian Renaissance style and begun in 1912 but not completed until 1932—the additional buildings surrounding the courtyard were added in 1936 and 1956. The Council Chamber is arranged in the Continental semi-circular style and the public can witness its sessions. The river terrace is the first part of a South Bank scheme which will one day give the public an uninterrupted riverside parade from Westminster to London Bridge. It already offers a superb view of the Houses of Parliament, the North Bank and the river traffic, and reaches as far as Waterloo Bridge.

Courtauld Institute Galleries, in Woburn Square, bring together for the first time in one superb display the important art collections bequeathed to London University. There is something for everyone here, but the real strength of this London gallery is the Courtauld collection of Impressionists and post-Impressionists and the Roger Fry collection. In the Courtauld collection are eight magnificent Cézannes and excellent examples of Manet, Gauguin, Seurat, Van Gogh and Renoir. The Fry collection shows much of this great critic's own work and is a curious and fitting memorial to his brave but now unfashionable Bloomsbury group of artist-craftsmen.

Covent Garden owes its name to the fact that hereabouts was an old garden of Westminster Abbey. The area was laid out by Inigo Jones as a residential neighbourhood. Inspired by the Piazza d'Arme at Livorno it was completed in 1638. In 1671, the piazza became a market in a small way by right of charter from the landowner, the Duke of Bedford. It is now our largest market for fruit, flowers and vegetables. The market is moving to Nine Elms in 1973. Meantime, at six in the morning Covent Garden is a gorgeous sight—especially when the spring flowers are in. Once produce was carried in wicker baskets. Its main work is over by 11 00. On the north side of the market is the **Royal Opera House,** built by Edward M. Barry in 1858 and incorporating statues and reliefs by Flaxman and Rossi which were on the previous theatre built on the site in 1808. At the west end of the market is **St. Paul's Church,** built in 1633 by Inigo Jones and described by him as 'the handsomest barn in England'. It is popularly known as the church 'with the front at the back'—the portico or seeming front is at the east end facing the market, the main entrance is at the west end. Its many memorials include those of Sir Peter Lely and Dame Ellen Terry. St. Paul's is the actors' church and also the Harvest Festival Church of the Market.

Crewe House is in Curzon Street, Mayfair—it was built by Edward Shepherd in 1735 for his own use. His name is commemorated in nearby Shepherd Market. Crewe House is a perfect example of the finest period of Georgian architecture and later became the town house of the Marquis of Crewe. The house is not open, but the lawns of its front garden and the severe but perfect proportions of its country-house architecture are a refreshing contrast to the insincerity of later styles that surround it.

Crosby Hall, on the Chelsea Embankment, was the Great Hall of Crosby Place, the fifteenth-century city home of Sir John Crosby, which once stood in Bishopsgate. Sir John Crosby was a Sheriff and later M.P. for the City and a prominent Yorkist friend of Edward IV. The Hall was moved to Chelsea in 1910 to save it from demolition. It is now incorporated into the buildings of the British Federation of University Women and fittingly is again in use as a Dining Hall. The Hall is of Reigate stone, and has a fine hammer-beam roof with Crosby's ram sign (he was a wool merchant) on each boss. The mediaeval central fireplace with the smoke vent in the roof can still be seen. The high table is Jacobean and much of the furniture Cromwellian. Behind the high table is one of the three copies of Holbein's 'Sir Thomas More's Family'. The original is lost, but copies were made for each of More's daughters.

Crystal Palace was re-erected at Penge in 1854 and was, until the disastrous fire of 1936, one of London's land-

marks. It originally housed the Great Exhibition of 1851 in Hyde Park, and was a masterpiece of cast iron and glass by Joseph Paxton. The only survivals of the Exhibition are the plaster prehistoric monsters on the islands in the boating lake in the south-west corner of the park. By the lake is a children's zoo. The park provides for sports and games and has some pleasant ornamental waters. An artificial ski slope is open in winter. The grounds contain the G.L.C.'s magnificent National Sports Centre, with a 12,000-seat stadium, covered sports hall, swimming bath and the King George VI Memorial Hostel.

Curiosities

CASTLE TAVERN in Cowcross Street, E.C.1, is the only public house in England with a pawnbroker's licence.

DUMMY HOUSEFRONTS were built at 23 and 24 Leinster Gardens, Bayswater, to preserve the street frontage when the Circle Line railway of London Transport was cut close to the road.

ELFIN OAK. A great favourite with the children, the Elfin Oak in Kensington Gardens (p. 56) was carved in 1930 by Ivor Innes from an old oak stump from Richmond Park. The tree was restored in 1966 and a tiny plaque gives credit for the work to fairies. It is no secret, however, that they had a great deal of help from Spike Milligan, the actor and producer.

GUARDS CRIMEA MEMORIAL in Waterloo Place (p. 117) carries figures of guardsmen cast from Russian cannon, and the guns piled at the rear were actually used by the Russians at Sebastopol.

NELSON'S TOMB in the crypt of St. Paul's (p. 93) is part of a magnificent monument prepared at Windsor for Cardinal Wolsey by Benedetto of Rovezzano. It was never completed, and the black marble sarcophagus was assigned to Nelson's tomb.

Cutty Sark at Greenwich is one of the world's most famous sailing ships and the only survivor of the speedy tea-clippers. These vessels, specially built for the Far East tea trade, sacrificed cargo space for speed, for the first ship home with the new crop gained rich rewards. From keel level in the dry dock look up at the graceful, yacht-like lines which gave her a best day's run of 363 miles.

On board is a museum of *Cutty Sark* and her contemporaries and a fine collection of figureheads.

Cutty Sark took her name from the short chemise of Robert Burns's witch 'Nannie' and the witch was her figurehead. The original figurehead by the famous John Hellyer was lost at sea. *Cutty Sark* was launched at

Dumbarton in 1869 and her sail spread was 32,000 square feet or ¾ acre.

Nearby another vessel, somewhat smaller and of more recent fame, has found a haven for retirement, the late Sir Francis Chichester's *Gipsy Moth IV*.

D

Dean's Yard, Westminster, is on the south-west side of Westminster Abbey and leads to some of the oldest parts of the Abbey itself, including the cloisters and the Jerusalem Chamber in which King Henry IV died. Both Westminster School (p. 121) and the Westminster Abbey Choir School adjoin Dean's Yard, and the green is used by both as a playing field.

Design Centre, in Haymarket, is the headquarters of the Design Council and presents to the public a cross-section of those products of British industry in all fields which are considered to be well designed. It is a constantly changing exhibition, supported by a valuable photographic reference library called 'Design Index' which was first displayed at the Festival of Britain in 1951. This was a progressive and almost revolutionary concept of the greatest interest both to traders and the general public.

Dickens House, at Doughty Street, Bloomsbury, was the home of Charles Dickens from early 1837 until late 1839. In it he wrote parts of the *Pickwick Papers*, *Oliver Twist*, *Nicholas Nickleby* and *Barnaby Rudge*. The house has a Dickens library and manuscripts, letters and other reminders of the novelist, and his study is still to be seen with the furniture and reading desk he used. In the basement is a reproduction of the Dingley Dell kitchen.

H.M.S. Discovery. This was the first vessel built in this country exclusively for use in scientific research under polar conditions. She was launched in 1901 and in the same year Captain Scott took her to Antarctica. He wanted her for the ill-fated expedition of 1910 but had to take *Terra Nova* instead.

Of the vessels permanently moored between Waterloo and Blackfriars bridges *Discovery* is the only one that allows the public on board. Scott's cabin is shown and in display cases are relics of his dash to the South Pole. It was on the return from the Pole that he and his four companions perished. The relics include letters and personal possessions of Scott, Bowers's 'Wrinkles in Practical Navigation' and a pitiful collection of stones. These were the geological specimens gathered at the South Pole which, when other equipment was abandoned, were dragged so many weary miles of the way home. They were found beside the bodies of Scott and his two remaining companions. H.M.S. *Discovery* is now used as a training ship for sea cadets.

Doggett's Coat and Badge. In honour of the accession of George I a Drury Lane actor-manager, one Thomas Doggett, endowed a rowing race in 1715 now known as the 'Watermen's Derby'. The first prize is a 'Coat of Orange Livery', a silver badge embossed with the prancing horse of the House of Hanover and a silver cup. The course is from London Bridge to Chelsea—about 4½ miles—and the competitors must be Thames watermen just out of their apprenticeship. The race is usually rowed on or about August 1st.

Downing Street, off White-hall, is named after its builder Sir George Downing who managed to hold office under Cromwell's Commonwealth and yet to be knighted by Charles II. Samuel Pepys, who was once his clerk, said of him: 'He is so stingy a fellow I care not to see him.' No. 10 has been the official town residence of the Prime Minister since the days of Sir Robert Walpole. No. 11 is now the official town residence of the Chancellor of the Exchequer, and No. 12 the office of the Government's Chief Whip. The houses are simple and dignified Georgian brick in pleasant contrast to the pretentious façade of the Foreign Office which faces them.

Down House, in the picturesque Kent village of Downe, was the home of Charles Darwin, the great Victorian naturalist. He lived and worked in the house for forty years, and died there in 1882. The memorial rooms on the ground floor, the gardens, the collection of Darwin relics, including the great man's panama and top hats and his experimental laboratory, are open to the public.

Drury Lane joins High Holborn to Aldwych and contains the Theatre Royal (the main entrance is in Catherine Street). The first theatre was opened there in 1663, and the present building was designed by Wyatt in 1812 with later additions in 1831 and alterations in 1922. Nell Gwyn is supposed to have sold oranges in the theatre before she became one of its actresses, and many of the great names of the English stage have since been associated with this celebrated building.

Duke of York's Column, in The Mall, was designed by Benjamin Wyatt and erected in 1833 to the memory of Frederick, Duke of York, who was the second son of George III. The statue of the Duke is a bronze by Westmacott. The Duke has no claim to fame other than his association with the nursery rhyme and his chronic impecuniosity—contemporary wags said that the Duke was placed so high in order to avoid his creditors, and others that the lightning conductor on his head was a spike for his bills. As the Duke had been Commander-in-Chief of the British Army, every soldier was stopped a day's pay in order to meet the cost of his memorial— he was unpopular both in life and in death.

Dulwich still retains the atmosphere of a village although it is surrounded by South London suburbia—it even boasts the last toll-gate in London. In the spring the rhododendrons and azaleas in its park are magnificent. It has retained its rural charm, thanks to the benefactions of Edward Alleyn (1566–1626) who was a wealthy Shakespearian actor and bear-baiter. He was the founder of the College of God's Gift which, in the nineteenth century, was re-established as Dulwich College and Alleyn's School. **Dulwich College Picture Gallery** was London's first public art gallery (1814) and was designed by Sir John Soane. The collection contains excellent examples of the works of Cuyp, Rembrandt, Rubens, Van Dyck, the two Teniers, Poussin, Watteau, Reynolds and Richard Wilson.

E

Earl's Court Exhibition, at the west end of Earl's Court Station, was the largest reinforced concrete building in the world when it was completed in 1937. It was to the design of C. Howard Crane on a site devoted to exhibitions since the celebrated shows of Buffalo Bill in 1887. The arena can be converted at the operation of a lever into a large indoor swimming pool. Earl's Court is the home of such exhibitions as the Motor Show, the Royal Tournament and the Royal Smithfield Show.

Eltham Palace, in Woolwich, was from the time of Edward II to Henry VIII one of the principal royal palaces. The Palace was ruined by the Parliamentarians, but the fifteenth-century Great Hall and the stone bridge which spanned the moat survive. The hammer-beam roof of the hall should certainly be seen, but it is in its associations that Eltham so fascinates—here Richard II's quarrel with Gloucester came to a head, and here Henry VIII spent much of his boyhood.

Ely Place is a private cul-de-sac off Charterhouse Street whose name, together with the ancient Church of St. Etheldreda (p. 89), is all that remains of the mediaeval town palace of the bishops of Ely. Most of the 'liberties' inherited from the bishops are gone, but a beadle on duty night and day in the Lodge in the middle of the road at the

gate entrance is, so far, an obstinate survival.

Embankment usually refers to the Victoria Embankment which runs along the north side of the Thames between Westminster and Blackfriars Bridges. It is a fine walk, or a delightful bus ride, of about 1½ miles, with excellent views of London's finest bridges, of the river traffic, and of St. Paul's at one end and of the Clock Tower of Big Ben at the other. From Westminster Bridge to the Temple are gardens where in summer the bands play and open-air teas are popular. Here in early summer the G.L.C. holds its annual open-air Art Exhibition, bringing the flavour of Paris's Left-Bank to London. In the gardens near Charing Cross Station is the beautiful York Gate designed by Balthasar Gerbier as the water gate of the old York House, the home of Charles I's friend, the ill-fated Duke of Buckingham. The site marks the original river bank before the Embankment was built between 1864 and 1870. The river wall is of granite, eight feet thick. Four ships are permanently moored to the Embankment—H.M.S. *President* and H.M.S. *Chrysanthemum*, both First World War sloops and now the headquarters of the London Division of the R.N.R., H.M.S. *Discovery* of Antarctic fame (p. 27), and the *Wellington*, a Second World War frigate, now the floating Livery Hall of the Honourable Company of Master Mariners. Among many memorials along the

Embankment the most famous are Cleopatra's Needle
(p. 21), and the Boadicea Memorial on the corner of
Westminster Bridge (p. 10).

Epping Forest, in Essex, extends from
Wanstead Flats and Highams Park to
the town of Epping—more than 10
miles long and 2 miles wide at its widest
part. Its 5,800 acres are all that remain
of the old forest of Waltham, which 300
years ago covered 60,000 acres and was
a forest in the original meaning of the
word—untilled land over which the
crown had hunting rights.

It is still easy to get lost in its thick woods of oak,
beech, hornbeam, birch, and holly. In the heart of this
vast expanse, far from the noise of traffic, the observant
(and lucky) may even today glimpse a black fallow
deer, or badger, fox, weasel or stoat, as well as squirrels
and rabbits.

On most days of the year you can hire a boat on
Connaught Water; there is public golf at Chingford, an
open-air swimming pool at Whipps Cross, funfairs on
public holidays on Wanstead Flats and Chingford
Plain, and, of course, there is still plenty of open space
for cricket and football. A forest museum is housed in
Queen Elizabeth's Hunting Lodge, Chingford, a unique
building which has a Tudor timber roof to its Banqueting
Room.

Epsom, in Surrey, is a defiantly country town refusing to
be included in a sprawling London. It was a fashionable
spa in Stuart times and Charles II held court there. It has
long been associated with horse racing and training, and
on Epson Downs, to the south, is the world's most
famous racecourse. The Derby has been run here (in
honour of the twelfth Earl of Derby) since 1780—it
usually takes place in early June. But Epsom Downs
afford pleasure to thousands the year round—they

provide free walking over glorious country to the woodier hills of Dorking and beyond. Epsom Salts are magnesium sulphate, first obtained from Epsom springs.

Fat Boy is a cherub-like gilded figure high on the wall of Cock Lane at the junction with Giltspur Street which links Old Bailey and Smithfield. It commemorates the northernmost spot reached by the Great Fire of 1666.

Fenton House, in Hampstead, was built in 1693 of red brick, and now houses the Benton Fletcher collection of early keyboard instruments. It includes British and European harpsichords, virginals and spinets of the sixteenth to the eighteenth centuries beautifully kept and still in use for the training of students. The house also contains the Binning Collection of Furniture and Porcelain and a Constable painting of Hampstead Heath. The garden is as delightful as the house and its contents.

Festival Gardens, in Battersea Park, were first designed as the lighter side to the London section of the 1951 Festival of Britain. Clearly inspired by the Tivoli Gardens in Copenhagen, they convert the river front of Battersea Park into an enchanting pleasure garden and a modern Fun Fair. The Gardens remain pleasure gardens—beautifully laid out and equally brilliant by night and day.

Fleet Street, 'the street of ink', is as old as English printing. Caxton's assistant Wynkyn de Worde had his printing press 'at London in Fletestrete at the signe of the Swane'. It was named from the Fleet River, which still flows underground from Hampstead and at low tide can be seen entering the Thames through a conduit beneath Blackfriars Bridge. All the great national and provincial newspapers have offices in or near Fleet Street, and its historic buildings include the Cock Tavern and the Cheshire Cheese (both seventeenth-century) and the Church of St. Dunstan-in-the-West, with a contemporary statue of Queen Elizabeth I on its south wall. At No. 1, 'at the sign of the Marygold at Temple Bar', is Child's Bank which claims to be the earliest established bank in London (mid-seventeenth-century).

Forty Hall is a handsome seventeenth-century mansion splendidly restored by the Enfield Borough Council. The house contains some good period furniture and a small local museum. There are several lavishly decorated plaster ceilings. A magnificent courtyard and stable block provide refreshments, and there is a gallery for loan exhibitions. Forty Hall stands in parkland, surrounded by great cedars, with a lake before its main door.

Foundling Hospital, in Brunswick Square, Bloomsbury, now called the Thomas Coram Foundation for Children, was founded by Captain Thomas Coram in 1739 for the care of deserted children. In 1926 the Hospital moved to Berkhamsted, but the site was preserved and 'Coram's Fields' are still a children's playground. The hospital's association with art began in its earliest days when Hogarth painted the portrait of its founder and persuaded fellow artists to present works of art for sale with a view to attracting revenue to the charity. In the days of George II the resulting **Art Gallery** was quite a fashionable rendezvous. The present Court Room is an exact replica of the old, and much of the original panelling and plaster work has been re-installed. There are paintings by Hogarth, Reynolds, Kneller, Gainsborough, and Millais and a Raphael cartoon. There is sculpture by Rysbrack and Roubiliac.

Freemasons' Hall, in Great Queen Street, off Kingsway, is the home of English freemasons throughout the world and the headquarters of the United Grand Lodge of

England. The building (architects Ashley and Newman) was completed in 1933 as a war memorial to freemasons.

Free Tickets for television and radio concerts and shows can be obtained from the BBC Radio and TV Ticket Unit, Broadcasting House, W1A 1AA. You must apply in writing, enclosing a stamped addressed envelope; preferably well in advance and stating a choice of programmes in order of preference. Similar tickets are available from the commercial television companies— you should telephone 01-953 6100, 01-902 8846 or 01-387 9494 for details. It is possible to visit the Fleet Street newspaper offices and works for evening visits, but there are long waiting lists and you must give as much notice as possible. The Post Office buildings in London may be visited—please see the 'How to Get There' section of this book for details.

Friends' House, opposite Euston Station, is the headquarters of the Society of Friends, commonly known as 'The Quakers'. It is a dignified building by H. Lidbetter, erected in 1926. Among many treasured possessions of the Society is the original journal of George Fox, the founder, and the library is the finest Quaker library in the world.

Fulham Palace is the official residence of the Bishop of London. The oldest part of the present structure is the great quadrangle built by Bishop FitzJames in the early sixteenth century—the rest of the buildings are eighteenth- and nineteenth-century. Part of the ancient moat is now in a public park known as the Moat Garden. Between the Palace and the Thames is **Bishop's Park** which was originally part of the Palace grounds. The terrace embankment is an excellent vantage point for watching the river traffic and especially the start of the Oxford and Cambridge Boat Race (p. 8).

On the Fulham side of Putney bridge is **All Saints' Church,** and although the present fabric by Sir Arthur Blomfield dates only from 1880, it preserves older features of great interest. The tower dates from 1440 and contains a peal of ten bells—six of which were installed in 1549 and recast in 1729. The interior is rich in monuments and brasses, including an authentic Grinling Gibbons memorial to a Dr. Barrow who was a good friend to Milton. The font dates from 1622. Ten Bishops of London and two Lord Mayors are buried in the churchyard, but it is the tombstone of Joseph and Isabella Murr which attracts most attention. The upper half eulogizes Isabella at some length; the lower half, left presumably for the virtues of Joseph, bears three words—'He's gone too'.

Gardening Centre. Alongside the glories of Adam-decorated Syon House (p. 104) is the Gardening Centre, 55 resplendent acres permanently exhibiting the very choicest products of the horticultural 'industry', set in 'Capability' Brown's park. There are woodland gardens, lakeside walks, spectacular sub-tropic displays and a fantastic summer array of over 12,000 roses. If this is how you see your garden (any millionaire of genius could do it) there are experts to advise you, a shop to start you off, and refreshments (from a quick cup of tea to a gastronomic experience) to keep you going.

Geffrye Museum in Kingsland Road, Shoreditch, is a fascinating collection of furniture arranged in chronological order as specimen rooms from 1600 to the present day. Each room is very efficiently catalogued on well-designed notice boards. The museum is appropriately placed in the heart of Shoreditch furniture manufacturing area, and is housed in a block of charming almshouses built in 1715 with funds from a bequest of Sir Robert Geffrye who was a master of the Ironmongers' Company and Lord Mayor of London in

1685. It provides an exhibition hall, a reference library and a collection of wood and ironwork to assist students who can also call on the staff for technical advice on handicrafts. Although it is a specialist establishment of great interest to adults, the museum takes a particular interest in children. Local schoolchildren can attend regularly for handicraft classes or other activities, while parties come from all over the south of England as part of social history courses. The captions to exhibits are interesting and attractively devised and children are encouraged both to take notes and to ask questions.

Gentlemen-at-Arms are one of the two royal body-guards—the other is the Yeomen of the Guard (p. 123). The Honourable Corps of Gentlemen-at-Arms was first formed in 1509 and today is composed of about thirty ex-officers of the Army and Royal Marines with distinguished service. The Captain is a political appointment changing with each government. The uniform is magnificent and is modelled on that of the Life Guards in the 1850s—gilt helmet with swans' feathers, scarlet tail coats, gold epaulettes, cross and waist belts, white gauntlets, gold striped trousers and Wellington boots. All carry swords, officers carry sticks, the gentlemen carry pole-axes—as long as a lance with spike at tip and an axe on the side. At most state functions Gentlemen-at-Arms and Yeomen of the Guard are in attendance.

Geological Museum, in Exhibition Road, South Kensington, is primarily a museum for the student of geology and mineralogy but of interest to anyone who wishes to understand the scenery or these islands, or to make his scrambles over fell, moor, downlands or highlands more interesting. Opened in Autumn 1972 by H.M. The Queen was 'The Story of the Earth', a major new exhibition relating the history of our planet from its cosmic origins to the earth as we know it today.

George Inn, off Borough High Street, Southwark, is London's last galleried hostelry. Rebuilt after a fire in 1677, it was once an important coaching inn for travellers to and from the Channel ports. The double tier of wooden galleries once extended round the whole inn yard—they were the only means of access to the bedrooms. It is possible that Shakespeare knew the George, and it is certain that Dickens knew it well.

Golders Hill, at Golders Green, is a separate small park which is a westerly extension of Hampstead Heath. It was originally the grounds of a large house at the main entrance, and has a pretty lake, a charming old-English garden, and a variety of animals in enclosures.

Grange Farm Camp, at Chigwell in Essex, is set in beautiful country overlooking the Roding valley towards Epping Forest. The Camp was first opened in its present form for the Festival of Britain in 1951, and there are excellent amenities for campers and provision for outdoor sports of all kinds, including open-air swimming pools. There is generally tent or hut accommodation, with or without meals, for parties of adults and children wishing to stay one night or more. Grange Farm is an admirable addition to the pleasures of London's countryside.

Gray's Inn, in Holborn, is one of the four remaining Inns of Court and its mediaeval origins are in some dispute. Its buildings, now fully restored in harmony with surviving architecture, retain the dignity of the old, and its quadrangles and gardens, where Pepys and Addison walked, are a delight. The Elizabethan hall has been skilfully rebuilt and work on the library is also completed. Charles Lamb could write of the gardens 'they are still the best gardens of the Inns of Courts, my beloved Temple not forgotten'. A tribute to Gray's Inn's most famous son—Francis Bacon, Lord Verulam, who laid out most of the grounds—is his statue in South Square, and in the gardens is the catalpa tree which he is reputed to have planted. The gatehouse in High Holborn dates from 1688 and is where Dryden's publisher, Jacob Tonson, had his book shop.

Green Park was added to St. James's Park by Charles II. It is a simple tree-studded grassland which has become a restful haven from the roar of Piccadilly or from the pavements of The Mall. At Hyde Park Corner is the Wellington Arch designed by Decimus Burton (1828), surmounted by a large bronze quadriga by Adrian  Jones representing Peace (1912), and containing in its base the smallest police station in London. The ornamental wrought-iron gates on the Piccadilly side of the park were taken from the old Devonshire House.

Greensted. A mile to the west of Chipping Ongar, along an elm-lined avenue, is the tiny church of St. Andrew, Greensted. It is our only surviving wooden Anglo-Saxon Church and is built of great oaks, untrimmed except for bark-stripping, halved and set up alongside each other like a stockade. The shingled spire is seventeenth century, and a painted panel inside the church illustrates the martyrdom of St. Edmund, a king of the East Angles, whose body rested here in 1013 on its way to re-burial at what is now Bury St. Edmunds.

Greenwich, some six miles down river from London Bridge, has been closely associated with Britain's sea-power since the days of the Tudors. The best approach is by river launch from Westminster pier—getting a waterman's view of the Greater London Council's Pepys Estate, built where Henry VIII made his chief

naval dockyard. Tradition has it it was near here
Elizabeth I walked over Raleigh's cloak. Rum ware-
houses incorporated in the new building embody
another seafaring tradition. A very full day's outing to
Greenwich would include the Royal Naval College
(p. 85), the National Maritime Museum (p. 72), the
Queen's House (p. 81), the Old Royal Observatory
(p. 85), Greenwich Park, *Cutty Sark* and the late Sir
Francis Chichester's *Gipsy Moth IV* (p. 26), St. Alfege's
Church, the Theatre and Art Gallery, Blackheath (p.
7), and Morden College (p. 70).

Grosvenor Square lies to the south of the west end of
Oxford Street—it was originally laid out by Sir Richard
Grosvenor (an ancestor of the Duke of Westminster) in
1695, and is one of London's most impressive squares.
During the Second World War it became known as
'Little America'. The U.S.A. Embassy designed by
Saarinen and surmounted by a giant eagle, surprisingly
dwarfed by the massive gilded front, now fills the west
side of the Square. The old Embassy was at No. 1 and
here too, during the Second World War, was the H.Q. of
the U.S. Command in Europe. At No. 20, General
Eisenhower had his H.Q., and almost the whole square
was occupied by various American services. At the
Grosvenor Chapel (1730), just off the square in South
Audley Street, a tablet commemorates the association of
American services with the Church. But the best symbol
of the U.S.A. is in the Square's gardens—the bronze
statue of President F. D. Roosevelt by Sir William Reid
Dick. It was unveiled by Mrs. Roosevelt in 1948. But
these are modern American associations; in 1785 John
Adams, who succeeded George Washington as President
came to represent the young U.S.A. at No. 9.

Guards. The Guards Division are an integral and colourful part of the London scene, and without going into
too much technicality it is worth knowing something of
their history and dress. The scarlet tunics and bearskin
caps are common to the Guards Division as a whole, but

the following details will suffice to distinguish the separate regiments:

	Hatband	Bearskin	Buttons
Grenadiers	Scarlet	White goat-hair plume on left	Set singly
Coldstream	White	Scarlet plume on right	Set in pairs
Scots	Red, white and blue diced	No plume	Set in threes
Irish	Green	Pale blue feather plume on right	Set in fours
Welsh	Black	White, green and white feather plume on left	Set in fives

The bearskin became the common head-dress after the defeat of the French Imperial Guard by the Grenadiers at Waterloo. The Grenadiers and the Coldstreamers are the only regiments of the Division privileged to march through the City of London 'with bayonets fixed, drums beating and colours flying'. The 'Time Beater' of the Grenadiers (the drummer on the right flank) still wears black arm bands in mourning for Charles II. They were formed in 1656. The Coldstreamers are so named from the village of Coldstream in the Border country where the regiment was stationed when its Cromwellian General Monck ordered it south to join Charles II at the Restoration. The Scots Guards were first formed in 1642, the Irish Guards in 1900, and the Welsh Guards in 1915. The Guards in London are quartered at Chelsea Barracks. In addition to guard duties at Buckingham Palace, St. James's Palace and Clarence House, a night guard is provided for the Bank of England. For Changing the Guard see page 16.

Guildhall is just off Cheapside—it dates from the early fifteenth century, but its site has been the centre of the City of London's local government for a thousand years.

Twice its mediaeval walls have survived when its roof has crashed in flames—once during the Great Fire of 1666 and again during the bombing of 1940. The Great Hall is the scene of City banquets, but it has other lesser ceremonials which the public can enjoy if they ask permission. On midsummer's day, for example, a husting is erected at the east end of Great Hall, and there the Sheriffs of the City are elected in a picturesque and colourful ceremony, and in early November the new Lord Mayor is admitted to office with ancient ritual. In this same hall Lady Jane Grey was tried and condemned. There are two crypts—the eastern is open and this is the finest example of mediaeval groined vaulting in London. To the east of the Great Hall are the art gallery and the library. The library has the best collection of London prints in the country, and the art gallery has an interesting permanent collection on London and from time to time exhibits the work of London art groups and societies. The Guildhall Museum, temporarily housed nearby at Gillett House, Bassishaw High Walk, has important relics of Roman and mediaeval London including a head of Mithras found in 1954, and has given space to the Leathercraft Museum formerly at Leathersellers' College in Tower Bridge Road.

Gunnersbury Park is in Brentford. The two mansions date from the early nineteenth century and were once the home of the English Rothschilds. The park and gardens are well laid out and contain a 'Temple' which is all that remains of the original house designed by Webb in 1663. One of the mansions is now a museum.

H

Hadley. Nearly one mile north of High Barnet Station along the Great North Road is Hadley Green, site of the Yorkist victory in the Battle of Barnet on April 14th 1471. Nearby is the fifteenth-century parish church of

Monken Hadley (St. Mary's). The south-west turret of the embattled tower is surmounted by an eighteenth century cresset. This copper vessel was filled with oil and used as a beacon to rouse the neighbourhood in times of national emergency or celebration. The church contains many small brasses and some fine plate. Hadley Common (popularly known as Hadley Woods) stretches for almost 2 miles to Cockfosters Station. The area is the only unenclosed part of the once extensive Enfield Chase.

Ham Common, on the west side of Richmond Park and close to the river, is London's most rural common. Cows graze on the edge of the village cricket green; ducks waddle into the village pond; gorse, bracken, wild flowers, fine trees, and several village inns complete the picture. Some of the large houses round the Common are good Georgian, and a pleasant walk takes you to Ham House (see below) and the Thames towpath.

Ham House, on the river near Richmond, was originally built in 1610 for a courtier of James i, but its glories really began when it came by marriage into the possession of the Duke of Lauderdale—a favourite of Charles ii. The present mansion is very much as Lauderdale left it, and in an age of luxury and prodigal spending Ham House was one of the most lavish and talked-of houses in the country. Evelyn, the diarist, wrote that it was 'furnished like a great Prince's' and German, Dutch and Italian artists and craftsmen were brought over to decorate and elaborate its rooms and galleries. Today, Ham House is a section of the Victoria and Albert Museum, which has wisely retained the best of what remains of the original furniture and furnishings but has added many pieces from its own rich stores to fill in the gaps.

Hammersmith Mall. Both Lower Mall and Upper Mall, Hammersmith, have much charm and interest—they are terraces of Georgian houses by the river and include

Kelmscott House (1780) where William Morris lived and died and founded both his tapestry business and his printing press.

Hampstead, like so many suburbs of London, remains a village at heart. Its Church Row is a fine Georgian street leading to the Georgian church of St. John (1745). In the neighbouring graveyard are the tombs of many distinguished local dead, including John Constable, George and Sir Gerald du Maurier, and Sir Herbert Beerbohm Tree, Hampstead Grove, Holly Bush Hill, Fenton House (p. 33) and the quaint alleys nearby provide a village walk full of architectural interest. At the top of Heath Street, just below the Whitestone Pond, is a causeway which is used at week-ends throughout the summer for excellent open-air art shows. And down Downshire Hill is Regency England at its best with Keats House (p. 55) close by.

Hampstead Garden Suburb lies to the north-east of Golders Green Station and is an interesting example of suburban planning. It was laid out by Sir Raymond Unwin in 1907, and its church of St. Jude is a very controversial example of the ecclesiastical work of Sir Edwin Lutyens.

Hampstead Heath is a wild heathland, not too much tamed, for the pleasure of city dwellers, and included in it are the grounds of **Kenwood** with its mansion (p. 57) and its magnificent beech trees. The Heath's green hills, wooded dells and shaded lakes are only four miles from Charing Cross. Here Londoners can bathe in natural lakes or in a modern Lido, they can play improvised games on roomy grass or organized games on special grounds, they can roam as they please or run as trainers teach on cinder tracks, they can stroll or lie or ride, and in the winter they can sometimes toboggan and even ski, they can sail their model yachts, fly their kites or aeroplanes, or fish in solitude, or crowd to listen to the band. And at public holiday times (except at Christmas) they can let the world go hang and enjoy the famous Hampstead Fair. But there are other pleasures here—the pleasure of studying trees, grasses, wild flowers, birds and butterflies, the magnificent views from the Spaniards Road which crosses the Heath at its highest point (399 feet) and puts London at your feet with the Kent and Surrey hills as a backcloth to St. Paul's and the Houses of Parliament. There are the pleasant houses which fringe the Heath (and sometimes encroach), and, at week-ends, there is the Whitestone Pond for the sailing of boats. They say Dick Turpin, the highwayman, frequented  the Spaniards Inn where the old Toll Gate house still remains, and on the northern edge you can still go singing 'Down at the Old Bull and Bush'. On the edge of the Heath, near the Whitestone Pond, is the 'Vale of Health'. The origin of the name is uncertain; if it refers to the once-fashionable (and curative) Hampstead Spa nearby, it must be noted that the spa's heyday was well before the marsh was drained in 1777. On the whole it seems most likely that the Hampstead Water Company, which drained this waterlogged spot, gave it its inspired name to help it live down its insalubrious past.

Hampton Court Palace was built between 1515 and 1520 for Cardinal Wolsey as his personal residence, and was taken over by Henry VIII after the Cardinal's fall. Henry greatly enlarged and enriched the palace and brought five of his wives in turn to live there as Queen. Charles I lived there in power and as a prisoner, but added nothing to the structure. William and Mary made major alterations—preserving the Tudor fabric but adding the superb Fountain Court and Garden Front by Sir Christopher Wren. The Palace nowadays is used in part for 'grace and favour' residences allotted by the Crown, but the main buildings are open to the public all or part of the year (see How to Get There section).

Walk through the second courtyard and see the curious astronomical clock over the Anne Boleyn gateway made for Henry by Nicholas Oursian in 1540; see Henry's Great Hall with its magnificent hammer-beam roof; discuss the taste of Charles II in the portraits of his ladies round the State Apartments; realize the domestic economy problems of a great palace in the Tudor kitchens and pantries; and admire the Great Vine—said to have been planted in 1769 and now proud of a main branch 100 feet long. But having seen so much you still cannot leave without enjoying the gardens—there is nowhere in England where the herbaceous borders are more luxuriant, and the lawns and lily ponds more beautifully planned. For the really energetic, and the children, there is finally the Maze of close-clipped hedges 6 feet high and 2 feet thick—probably planted in the time of William III.

Hampton Court is England's most beautiful and most interesting royal palace.

Harefield is just north of Uxbridge in the most rural part of Middlesex. Its church of St. Mary, south of the village, contains a collection of sepulchral monuments 'worthy to be ranked with the richest English parish churches'. The chancel is thirteenth-century and the principal monuments are to Alice, Countess of Derby (1636), and to many of the Newdigate and Ashby families dating from the fifteenth to the late eighteenth century. Between church and village are the Countess of Derby's almshouses.

Harrow can boast not only of its famous public school but also of one of the finest thirteenth-century churches in the south of England, with an exceptionally beautiful nave and many fine brasses. The churchyard looks over many miles of countryside—Harrow Hill is 400 feet above sea level. Harrow School was established in 1574 by one John Lyon, who left land and money for the maintenance of the school, to help scholars at the universities, and 'for the releyffe of the poore'. The school buildings are clustered round the top of Harrow Hill, and for the most part they have no architectural distinction—they date from the late nineteenth century. The War Memorial Building has greater interest—it was built in 1921 and leaves Victorianism far behind. Harrovians wear flat straw hats, and among many great names in the School's registers are those of Byron, Peel, Palmerston and Churchill.

Haymarket Theatre has been one of London's Theatres Royal (see Drury Lane) since 1767. It was founded in 1720 and rebuilt by Nash in 1821. The portico is one of the most elegant in London.

Hayward Gallery. Named after a former London County Council Leader, this London Home for Arts Council exhibitions is part of the South Bank Arts Centre (p. 98). Air-conditioned and perfectly lit, the gallery is on two levels with three open-air sculpture courts. The size and number of exhibitions can be varied by the use of partitions.

Heathrow Airport is one of the busiest of all international airports and the third most important port of any kind in Britain. Here you can spend a rewarding day as a sightseer, capturing some of the romance and mystery of faraway places. The public enclosure is a roof garden, where the visitor is given a running commentary on arrivals and departures. On the southern side of the airport, a vast new cargo terminal has been built.

Near the control tower is the world's first inter-denominational airport chapel, St. George's. Sited underground for sound insulation and to avoid a clash of architectural styles, the simple, circular cave-like chapel is a place of peace amongst noise and bustle.

The airport is linked to Hounslow West Underground by express bus service A.1. Work has also started on the extension of the Piccadilly Line to the airport.

Highgate is still an eighteenth-century village in spite of the modernity of its High Point flats. In The Grove at No. 3 is the house where Coleridge died (he is buried in the church nave). Highgate School, nearby, was founded in 1565. In Swain's Lane is the **Cemetery** whose fantastic catacombs and family vaults hold many distinguished Londoners, and whither left-wing enthusiasts make pilgrimage to honour the very bourgeois tomb of Karl Marx. A little way down Highgate Hill is **Waterlow Park** which was the garden of the house of Sir Sydney

Waterlow, and in whose grounds is Lauderdale House, which once belonged to the first Duke of Lauderdale, who was one of Charles II's ministers. Nell Gwyn was installed here, much to the annoyance of the poet and wit, Andrew Marvell (1621–78), who lived in a nearby cottage. Sir Sydney's bronze statue in the park should be seen in London rain—it carries a bronze umbrella.

Hogarth's House, in Chiswick, was the country villa of the painter William Hogarth (1697–1764) who lived there from 1749 to 1764 and left it for his town house at Leicester Fields (now demolished) only when he knew he was dying. His body was taken back to Chiswick and is buried in the churchyard of St. Nicholas, where the tomb still stands. The house was opened in 1904 as a Hogarth Museum; it is a typical example of Queen Anne architecture.

Holland House, in Kensington, is the only remaining 'country seat' in what is now central London. It was built about 1605 and was known as Cope Castle after its first owner Sir Walter Cope. His son-in-law became first Earl of Holland in 1629 but was beheaded in the civil war. In the eighteenth and early nineteenth centuries the estate belonged to the Fox family who adopted the Holland title. This was its heyday, when all politicians and writers of the Whig persuasion made it their headquarters. A modern Youth Hostel has been built alongside the restored east wing. The park, where open-air concerts are held in summer, has a very attractive garden.

Honourable Artillery Company has its headquarters at Armoury House in City Road, Finsbury. It is the oldest regiment in the British Army. Its actual origin is unknown, but Henry VIII undoubtedly granted it a Charter in 1537. The Charter was addressed to 'The Fraternity or Guild of St. George' and charged it to practise 'the science and feat of shooting' with the bow and changed its name to 'The Fraternity or Guild of Artillery of Longbows Crossbows and Handguns'. The present building dates from 1735 and is stored with fascinating military relics and records. The Regiment has the right to furnish a Guard of Honour when royalty visits the City, and the right to march through the City 'with bayonets fixed, drums beating and colours flying'. The H.A.C. also fires all salutes from the Tower of London (p. 109). It is typical of England that the H.A.C.—the oldest of our regiments—is nowadays a voluntary body of the Army Volunteer Reserve. It is also the pride of the City of London.

Horniman Museum, in Forest Hill, was presented to London by Mr. F. J. Horniman. It has a magnificent collection of early tools, a fascinating array of dance masks and totems in its Magic and Religion section, an aquarium, and, during the summer, a glass beehive showing a bee colony in active production. There is also a fine collection of musical instruments and the library is invaluable to any student of man's first beginnings and subsequent development. The architecture is an interesting specimen of the *art nouveau* style by C. Harrison Townsend (1902).

Horse Guards is the name given to the beautifully proportioned building designed by William Kent in 1753 on the site of the guard house to the old Palace of Whitehall. The building now houses government offices, but a mounted guard is still posted (p. 16). Horse

Guards Parade, approached through the central archway, is the site of the tilt-yard of the old Palace, and here on the sovereign's official birthday the ceremony of 'Trooping the Colour' takes place. The sovereign leads a parade of the Guards—both horse and foot—resplendent in their full dress uniforms. It is a magnificent spectacle in scarlet, blue, silver and gold, against the green background of St. James's Park and the pearly grey Portland stone of the Horse Guards itself.

Horticultural Halls. The Old Hall is in Vincent Square, Westminster, and is the headquarters of the Royal Horticultural Society. The New Hall is in Greycoat Street. Visitors interested in horticulture should watch out for the many flower shows held in these halls.

Hospitals. London has many general and specialist hospitals, but the following are the oldest and most famous:

St. Bartholomew's at Smithfield (colloquially known as 'Barts') is the oldest hospital in London on its original site. It was originally part of the Augustinian priory founded by the monk Rahere in 1123. It is a parish in its own right with the charming eighteenth-century church of St. Bartholomew-the-Less within the precincts.

The Gateway dates from 1702 and in the Great Hall are some good eighteenth-century portraits.

Guy's, near London Bridge Station, was first endowed in 1721 by a miserly bookseller named Thomas Guy, who was reputed to have made a fortune from South Sea stock. The sculpture on the present façade is the work of John Bacon (1773).

London, in the Whitechapel Road, was founded in 1758 and has the largest out-patients' department in England.

St. George's, at Hyde Park Corner, is an excellent example of severe Georgian architecture—it was founded in 1733 and the present buildings are largely the work of William Wilkins (1829).

St. Thomas's was first founded at Southwark in 1213, but was transferred to its present site opposite the Houses of Parliament on the south bank of the Thames in 1868. The St. Thomas was Thomas Becket, the chancellor-archbishop murdered at the instigation of Henry II. The new buildings are in the grandest modern manner.

Household Cavalry. The Corps of Household Cavalry comprises two separate regiments—The Life Guards with scarlet tunics and white plumed helmets, and The Blues and Royals with blue tunics and red plumed helmets. The Life Guards originated in a body of cavaliers who were the bodyguard of Charles I during the Civil War, and The Blues and Royals (formerly the Royal Horse Guards) in a Cromwellian regiment of horse. Both regiments share the honour of providing a personal bodyguard for the sovereign on all state occasions, and the Changing of the Guard (p. 16) is London's most popular daily free spectacle.

House of St. Barnabas-in-Soho. This Georgian house is an elegant feature of a not very elegant area. You may view its magnificent interior with its wrought-iron balustrading, elaborate ceilings and fireplaces and a pretty 'crinoline' staircase. There is an early Victorian chapel and an ancient mulberry tree in the small paved garden.

Houses of Parliament, or more correctly the Palace of Westminster, was a royal residence from the days of Edward the Confessor until Henry VIII was presented with the neighbouring Whitehall Palace. The old Westminster Palace was almost totally destroyed by fire in 1834, and Parliament is now housed in the impressive neo-Gothic creation of Sir Charles Barry and Pugin, which was begun in 1840 and opened in 1852.

Fortunately, the original **Westminster Hall** was saved from the fire. First built by William Rufus in 1097 it was rebuilt by Richard II in 1398. Its famous hammer-beam roof of oak has the unrivalled span of nearly 70 feet, and beneath it have been enacted some of the most stirring scenes in British history—here Sir Thomas More, Charles I, Warren Hastings, and many more, have stood their trial.

Big Ben is the bell which strikes the hours dictated by the Palace Clock (23 ft. in diameter) in its 320-ft. Tower. It is named after Sir Benjamin Hall, who was Commissioner of Works in 1858 when it was installed. The first stroke of Big Ben is exactly on the hour.

To view the House of Commons or the House of Lords either in or out of session the best method is to write to your M.P., but you can queue for admission without tickets. Admission to Westminster Hall and the Lobby is easy at most times. When the House is in session a Union Jack flies from the Victoria Tower during the day and at night a light shines in the Clock Tower above Big Ben.

In the gardens of the Victoria Tower is the impressive bronze group of the Burghers of Calais by Rodin.

Hyde Park was once the ancient Manor of Hyde and is now London's most famous park. At the Marble Arch corner is the world's freest debating society, where any orator of any creed, colour or persuasion may have his say. Near the Achilles Statue (made from guns taken by Wellington, and not of Achilles but a copy of one of the horse-tamers on the Monte Cavallo at Rome) the bands play in season. Along Rotten Row (perhaps originally *route du Roi*) the riders show their skill—or lack of it— summer and winter. To the north of the Serpentine is the bird sanctuary adorned with Epstein's 'Rima'—a memorial to W. H. Hudson whose *Green Mansions* breathes all his love of nature—and at Bowater House at the Knightsbridge entrance is his controversial group 'Pan'. On the Serpentine you may boat or sail, in it you may bathe at London's first Lido established by George Lansbury, and separating it from the lake in Kensington Gardens is the beautiful stone bridge built by Sir John and George Rennie in 1826. But there are acres of grass and woodland where you may just do nothing but think how easy it is to forget that you are in the centre of a great city.

Hyde Park Corner, at the west end of Piccadilly, is over-looked by the Wellington Arch and the Wellington Museum (p. 118). There is a bronze equestrian statue of the Duke facing his old home, and war memorials of the Royal Artillery by C. S. Jagger (1928). On the north side Decimus Burton's handsome Screen forms the entrance to Hyde Park, and an underpass speeds through traffic between Knightsbridge and Piccadilly.

I

Imperial War Museum is in the grounds of the Geraldine Mary Harmsworth Park in Lambeth, and was founded in 1917. The main building was originally designed as the Bedlam (Bethlehem) Hospital for the insane. The museum displays more than the engines of war and the means of defence; it is a fascinating visual record of the Commonwealth in action in two world wars. Its art collection has examples of most of our modern masters and its photographs and library are a treasure house for historians of today—and of tomorrow.

India House is one of the buildings which make up the imposing sweep of Aldwych. It is the London headquarters of the Republic of India and was built to the designs of Sir Herbert Baker in 1930. Externally, the architecture comprises with its western *milieu*, but internally it is unmistakeably oriental. There is a fine exhibition hall, a reference library and a reading-room.

Industrial Health and Safety Centre, at 97 Horseferry Road, Westminster, is an excellent display, administered by the Government, illustrating the contributions which modern inventions and devices can make to such problems as accident prevention, noise abatement, and the general safety and health of industrial workers. Expert advice is available to employers and employed.

Institute of Contemporary Arts belies its classical environment at Nash House in Carlton House Terrace (p. 90) by featuring all forms of today's (and tomorrow's) expression in the arts. Cinema, art gallery and bookstall under one elegant roof foster communication, and there are also lectures and discussions. Some of the Institute's activities are restricted to members, but the public are admitted to exhibitions and some other functions.

Jewel Tower. A mediaeval survival hiding behind Westminster Abbey, the Jewel Tower dates from 1365. With Westminster Hall it is all that remains of the old Palace of Westminster which from Edward the Confessor to Henry VIII was the principal royal residence. It was built to hold the private fortune of the king as distinct from the crown jewels and the treasury funds, and was used as such until the death of Henry VIII.

In the small vaulted rooms are display cases of pottery and other relics discovered during renovations and there is a section of the old timber foundations. The moat is now stocked with rainbow trout and goldfish.

Jewish Museum is at Woburn House, Tavistock Square. It contains many interesting relics of World Jewry illustrating the domestic and public worship of Jews. It includes early thirteenth-century Rams' Horns, an eighth-century Chanukah lamp, a sixteenth-century Venetian Ark of the Law and many scrolls.

Johnson's House. 'When a man is tired of London, he is tired of life', said Dr. Johnson. He lived in his house at 17 Gough Square close to the bustle of Fleet Street (p. 33) from 1748 to 1759, and there he compiled his great Dictionary. The house, quite apart from its literary associations, is a good example of Queen Anne domestic architecture.

Johnson's Summerhouse. This rustic, thatched summerhouse was originally at Streatham, where it was used by the great man when he took tea with Mrs. Thrale. Much-travelled since, it was faithfully restored by the Greater London Council and now looks quite at home in the shrubbery at Kenwood (p. 57).

K

Keats House. Wentworth Place, to give Keats House its correct name, is in Keats Grove, Hampstead. In this beautiful Regency house with its old-world garden Keats spent two of his five short creative years. Under the trees he wrote his immortal 'Ode to a Nightingale', and here he was nursed by his gracious neighbour Fanny Brawne. Finally he was compelled to sail for Italy in the care of his friend the artist Joseph Severn. In 1821, at the age of 25, Keats died of tuberculosis in Rome. Here in the Keats Memorial Museum, are many pathetic and fascinating relics of the poet, including the manuscript of his last work (the sonnet 'Bright Star') written in a blank page of his Shakespeare during the voyage to Italy, his last letter to Mrs. Brawne, and several portraits, including one of him on his death bed.

Kensington Gardens were once the private grounds of Kensington Palace. They were laid out in the early eighteenth century by Henry Wise and Charles Bridgman

and are now a public park especially devoted to children. On the west bank of the Long Water is Sir George Frampton's statue of Peter Pan— probably the most popular statue in London— and the Round Pond gives scope to ships' captains of all ages. But Kensington Gardens have much for the adult —long avenues of noble trees, the equestrian statue of Physical Energy by G. F. Watts, the sunken garden, the Flower Walk, the fountains and a pleasantly continental-looking open-air restaurant. The Albert Memorial (p. 2) is also in Kensington Gardens.

Kensington Palace, originally Nottingham House, was bought for the crown by William III and handed over to Sir Christopher Wren with instructions to turn it into a royal residence. He did his work admirably, and under George I William Kent completed it. The last sovereign to reside there was George II, but it was here that Princess Victoria was roused from her bed to hear of her accession. The Palace's main attractions are its Wren exterior and the **London Museum** (p. 64) now housed there. The Orangery (1704), long ascribed to Wren or Hawksmoor, most recently to Vanbrugh, has some excellent Grinling Gibbons carving.

Kenwood, Highgate, was the mansion (1767–8) and park of the Earl of Mansfield, one of our greatest Lords Chief Justice. Kenwood was presented to the nation by the late Lord Iveagh. It is a fine Georgian 'stately home' on the north-east corner of Hampstead Heath (p. 44). The

furniture and furnishings are contemporary with the house and the pictures include a magnificent self-portrait by Rembrandt, Vermeer's 'Guitar Player' and Gainsborough's 'Pink Lady'. The Library was designed by Robert Adam. In the stables, now converted into a pleasant restaurant, is the old family coach. From the garden terrace the lawns slope down to the water-lilied lake with its fake but most successful Georgian bridge on the left, the magnificent trees of Ken Wood itself in front, and colourful banks of rhododendrons on the right.

Kew Gardens are officially the Royal Botanic Gardens— the most famous botanical gardens in the world. They date from 1759 when a garden was specially laid out for Kew House. In 1841 the property was handed over to the state, and in 1897 Queen Victoria added the thatched **Queen's Cottage** and its woodland.

Kew Gardens are not a public park—their primary purpose is to serve the science of botany. Every year about 30,000 plants are identified, and information and specimens exchanged with experts all over the world. The Herbarium has over 7,000,000 dried plants and herbs, and the Library contains over 50,000 volumes. Research under cover goes hand in hand with the cultivation of over 45,000 different trees, shrubs and herbs in the open. It was here that the rubber tree of Brazil was prepared for the plantations of Malaya, and that Marquis wheat, which added thousands of square miles to the grain-bearing prairies in north-western Canada, was evolved.

For the ordinary visitor Kew is a paradise for shaded walks by the Thames or by the lake, for picnics by the Pagoda, or for the magnificent displays of spring flowers,

 of rhododendrons and azaleas in early summer, of fascinating cacti in their special scenic settings, of the jungles in the vast glass houses and of the Amazon water lily (*Victoria amazonica*) which in September produces a leaf six feet in diameter.

The pagoda was built by Sir William Chambers in 1761–2 and is a witness to the then fashionable interest in oriental décor. The Palm House was built to the design of Decimus Burton in 1848. The Flagpole near the Temperate House is 225 feet high—the tallest in the world—and is the main trunk of a giant Douglas fir from British Columbia. The Dutch House (or **Kew Palace**) is a red brick building near the northern end of Broad Walk and dates from 1631. King George III and Queen Charlotte used it and it contains some good period furniture.

Kingston-upon-Thames, in Surrey, takes its name from the Saxon Coronation Stone on which seven of our

Saxon kings are reputed to have been crowned. The stone is now placed outside the Guildhall. Kingston is an odd mixture of ancient and modern—a 'Royal' borough for 1,000 years with a post-war power station, a modern Guildhall with the Norman-built clattern bridge, and, as a further contrast, the quaint riverside and the ancient oaks of Richmond Park.

King's Troop, Royal Horse Artillery, has three special duties—ceremonial parades and firing of salutes (p. 94), publicizing the Army by musical drives and horsemanship displays, and maintaining the traditions of the Riding Establishment at Woolwich from which it sprang. The full-dress uniform is a hussar pattern jacket of blue, profusely decorated with gold piping, with breeches carrying a broad red stripe.

L

Lambeth Palace, by Lambeth Bridge, has been the London residence of the Archbishops of Canterbury for 700 years. The south gateway was built in 1499, and the Lollards' Tower about 1450. The buildings have suffered much from successive restorations and bombing, but they still retain their mediaeval flavour. The Great Hall has a good hammer-beam roof and now contains the library. The Guard Room, too, has a fine timber roof. Portraits of the archbishops from the sixteenth to the nineteenth century include the work of most of our great portrait painters from Holbein to Sargent. The crypt of the Chapel is the oldest part of the surrounding buildings and goes back to the early thirteenth century. The Lollards' Tower commemorates the followers of John Wycliffe, who argued his reforming faith with the Church of Richard II's day in this very palace. Near the south gateway is **St. Mary's Church**—it retains its late fifteenth-century tower and, as well as the tombs of some recent Archbishops, has the tomb of Admiral Bligh of the *Bounty* (1754–1817).

Lancaster House, in Stable Yard, beside St. James's Palace, dates from 1825. The Duke of York (p. 29) commissioned Benjamin Wyatt to design it, but the Duke died very much in debt before the house was finished. The Marquis of Stafford was a creditor and took over what therefore became Stafford House, which was completed by Robert Smirke and Charles Barry in 1840. The first Lord Leverhulme presented the house to the nation as a home for the London Museum and renamed it Lancaster House in honour of the sovereign's private dukedom and his own native county. It is now used for Government conferences and hospitality. The State Apartments are at times open to public view and their magnificence can be gauged by a remark of Queen Victoria when she was welcomed there by the Duchess of Sutherland—'I have come from my house to your palace'.

Law Courts is the unofficial name of the **Royal Courts of Justice.** The original architect—G. E. Street—died during their construction and Sir A. Blomfield completed them in a sentimental Victorian Gothic style. Nevertheless, the lofty central hall is well proportioned. The ceremony of paying **Quit Rents** is held at the Law Courts usually about 23rd October. It concerns the payment of rent for two pieces of land—the 'Moors' in Shropshire and the 'Forge' at St. Clement Danes— whose exact whereabouts are no longer known. For the Moors the Corporation of London pays a bill-hook and a hatchet. For the Forge the Corporation offers six horse shoes and sixty-one nails. The rents are accepted by the Queen's Remembrancer acting on behalf of the Crown. The public is admitted to this quaint historic ceremony.

Leadenhall Market, in Gracechurch Street, is over 600 years old, but the present building dates from 1881. Poulterers are still the main merchants but grocery and greengrocery businesses are well represented.

Lee Valley Regional Park is an exciting new recreational area now being developed in parts of the Lee Valley in

North East London. It is planned to make use of existing disused land, including gravel workings, so that a wide new range of leisure activities, including sailing, horse riding and golf, can be enjoyed. Pickett's Lock, a social centre with an exhibition hall and offering most sporting facilities, will be opened in Spring 1973.

Legal Procession. On the first day of the Michaelmas sittings after the Long Vacation, Her Majesty's Judges and Queen's Counsel attend a special service in Westminster Abbey and then move in colourful procession, the judges in ermine and scarlet, purple, or black and gold, Q.C.s in silk, all in full-bottomed wigs, to a reception given by their head, the Lord Chancellor, in the House of Lords.

Leicester Square is named from the second Earl of Leicester who built his house here in 1631. The Square was laid out in 1874 by Albert Grant and provided with the Shakespeare statue in the centre and busts of Newton, Reynolds, Hogarth and Hunter at its corners. It is a green and flowered oasis lit at night by the gay neon of cinema-land.

Leighton House, at 12 Holland Park Road, has an exotic interior built specially to the designs of Lord Leighton, and was his residence for thirty years until his death in 1896. It contains much fifteenth- and sixteenth-century Persian tiling and carving, an Arabian Hall with a fountain in the centre, many drawings and sculptures by Leighton, pictures by Burne-Jones, pottery by William de Morgan, and, in the entrance hall, a Tintoretto. In the studio are plaster casts of sections from the Parthenon Frieze and of a sculptured roundel of the Holy Family by Michelangelo. The small but interesting British Theatre Museum now has its home here.

Libraries. London has the finest library system in Great Britain. Each main suburban centre has its reference library with a wide range of books. Most of them have a specialized collection of local history, and each is responsible for its own sections of the Metropolitan Special Collection. The idea of this collection is that, by specialization, London as a whole should have a range of books far wider than the resources of any single library, used independently, could achieve. Hammersmith, for example, specializes in law and sociology, Fulham in Christianity and Holborn in transport and commerce.

Some of the local libraries are housed in buildings of interest in their own right, among them Pitshanger Manor (p. 78) and the Camden Library at Swiss Cottage designed by Sir Basil Spence.

Visitors particularly interested in the history of London will find the Guildhall library (p. 42) especially rewarding, while the visitor who wants a reference library for a quick consultation should probably choose the large Westminster Central Library just off Leicester Square.

Apart from these free public libraries, London has a large number of highly specialized libraries, belonging to companies, learned societies, colleges and other institutions. Many of these will, by arrangement but without charge, allow the public to use their facilities.

But the greatest library of them all is the huge domed Reading Room of the British Museum (p. 10), open only to holders of readers' tickets.

Lincoln's Inn, in Chancery Lane, is named from an Earl of Lincoln who established a law school in Shoe Lane in the fourteenth century. The records of the present Inn of Court go back to 1422. The chapel, attributed to Inigo Jones (1623), was extensively repaired by Wren in 1685. Its unique feature is the open undercroft or crypt where students and barristers 'walk and talk and confer for their learnings'. The Hall and Library are by Philip Hardwick (1843). The Gatehouse was originally erected in 1518 and Oliver Cromwell is said to have lodged there as a law student. The Old Hall, drastically restored in

1924–28, contains Hogarth's 'Paul before Felix'. The rolls of Lincoln's Inn include the names of More, Pitt, Walpole, Newman, Canning, Disraeli, Gladstone and Asquith.

Lincoln's Inn Fields lie between Kingsway and Lincoln's Inn—they were first laid out by Inigo Jones in 1618 and they soon became a recognized duelling ground. In 1683 Lord William Russell was executed there—a tablet marks the spot. The plane trees of the gardens are superb, and the surrounding houses show civic architecture at its best. On the north side is Sir John Soane's house (p. 96). On the south side is the Royal College of Surgeons (1835). Tennis courts, netball courts, leafy shade and green lawns make Lincoln's Inn Fields a perfect lunch-time strolling and recreation ground for city workers.

Little Stanmore, or Whitchurch, is near Edgware in Middlesex, where once stood the great mansion of Canons Park (so called because its site once belonged to the Augustinian canons) which was built for the Duke of Chandos (1715). The parish church has a fascinating interior built at the expense of the Duke in the early eighteenth century. Walls and ceilings are panelled and frescoed in the baroque manner, and behind the altar is a famous organ which Handel certainly knew and on which he probably played.

Lloyd's, the international market for insurance and world centre for marine and aviation news, is now in an impressive building in Lime Street, but it began as a coffee shop in 1689 and can be said to have 'happened' as a consequence of a Mr. Lloyd posting up snippets of shipping news for his business patrons. It was not until 1871 that Lloyd's was given official status by Act of Parliament. In 'The Room' (the underwriting room) hangs the Lutine Bell salvaged from the frigate *Lutine* which went down with nearly half a million pounds' worth of gold and specie off the Texel in 1799. The cargo was insured at Lloyd's and the liability was met in full. One stroke of the bell signals bad news, two strokes signal good news. 'A1 at Lloyd's' is known the world over as a guarantee of good faith.

London Museum was formerly housed in Lancaster House (p. 60), but since the war it has been transferred in smaller form to Kensington Palace. Here in beautiful rooms overlooking Kensington Gardens is an admirably arranged exhibition which tells the history of London from pre-history to modern times. The display includes fascinating illuminated dioramas of great events in London's story, an unrivalled collection of royal robes, and the dolls which Queen Victoria dressed and named when she lived here as a girl. The State Apartments, retaining the Queen Victoria relics and augmented by furniture and objects from the late Queen Mary's collection and her coronation robes, are now part of the Museum.

London School of Economics, off Aldwych, is a branch of the University of London, It was founded by Mr. and Mrs. Sidney Webb in 1895 and now has an international reputation. Its library of political and economic science is one of the largest in the world.

London Stone was for many years set in the street wall of St. Swithin's Church opposite Cannon Street Station and is now let into the wall of the new Bank of China building erected on the site. The stone is said to be the Roman milestone that once stood in Agricola's London forum. From it distances were measured along the great Roman military roads which radiated thence over the whole of Great Britain up to the Wall.

London's Wall. The two-mile long city wall built by the Romans around A.D. 200 enclosed a roughly oblong area along the Thames north bank from the Tower to Ludgate, taking in the north-west two sides of the slightly earlier Cripplegate fort. Remains of the wall, and mediaeval additions to it, can be seen, in the east, at the Tower itself, in Tower Hill Underground station (platform 1), beside the station in Wakefield Gardens and a few paces away behind Midland House in Cooper's Row; and, with the remains of the fort, towards the west end of today's 'London Wall' in St. Alphage Garden, beside St. Giles Cripplegate, in the underground car park, and along Noble Street. A stretch runs further west beneath the Post Office's King Edward Building. A 'marker' near the eastern end of today's 'London Wall' is the north wall of All Hallows church, which runs along the Roman wall line, with the vestry built on one of its bastions.

London Transport. The headquarters building in Broadway, Westminster, was designed in steel and Portland stone by Charles Holden, and completed in 1929—it is strutted above St. James's Park station. Thanks to the patronage of Frank Pick, the exterior is remarkable for its sculpture. On the north façade at first floor level is 'Night' and over the east façade 'Day'—both magnificent examples of the stone carving of Jacob Epstein. The eight bas-reliefs on the wings of the central block depict the winds—they are the work of Eric Gill, Henry Moore, F. Rabinovitch, Allan Wyon, A. H. Gerrard and Eric Aumonier. For travel enquiries, see page 111.

Lord Mayor's Show goes back to the sixteenth century when the Lord Mayor of London went to Westminster attended by the 'crafts in their best liveries' to present himself to the monarch. Today, the new Lord Mayor goes in his heavy and elaborate state coach (1756) accompanied by suitable pageantry to the Law Courts where he is received by the Lord Chief Justice as the

monarch's representative. The procession takes place annually on the second Saturday in November, and has each year a different theme, usually connected with the new Lord Mayor.

Lord's is the headquarters at St. John's Wood of the Marylebone Cricket Club (the M.C.C.) and of the Middlesex County Cricket Club. The M.C.C. was formed in 1787 from the White Conduit Cricket Club which played at Islington. Thomas Lord, their general factotum, acquired for them a cricket ground in Marylebone, and here the M.C.C. was born. Lord's is the cricketer's Holy Ground, redolent with the memories of Grace, Trumper, Ranjitsinhji, Hobbs, Bradman and Hutton. Visitors to the ground should take the opportunity to visit the Memorial Gallery, a cricket museum full of the history and romance of the game.

M

The Mall links Buckingham Palace (p. 12) and Trafalgar Square (p. 111), passing between St. James's Park (p. 90) and Green Park (p. 39). It is London's principal ceremonial driveway, as well as being an important traffic route. Its pink roadway and double avenue of limes are renowned. Many royal ceremonies now take place at Windsor, but there are still times when the Queen drives along The Mall with a jingling escort of Household Cavalry to meet distinguished visitors. On these occasions, and at the State Opening of Parliament (p. 101) and the Trooping the Colour Ceremony (p. 112), The Mall is decorated with flags and banners. Visitors who wish to see the Queen will find The Mall an excellent and not too crowded vantage point.

Mall Gallery is the home of the Federation of British Artists, originally formed by the Royal Society of Portrait Painters, The Royal Society of British Artists and The New English Art Club, but now embracing most of the major art societies. Exhibitions of the work of a number of art societies are held throughout the year, but the Federation also offers hospitality to many other exhibitions and occasionally to concerts.

Mansion House, at the Bank crossing, was built by George Dance the elder between 1739 and 1753. It is the official residence of London's Lord Mayor with a Corinthian portico from which he can watch civic and royal processions. As well as the private and official apartments it contains the Lord Mayor's tiny Court of Justice with cells beneath. Its chief reception room is the Egyptian Hall which is an impressive banqueting hall whose décor is somewhat debased classical Renaissance and not in the least Egyptian.

Marble Arch was originally designed by John Nash as the main gateway to Buckingham Palace. It was found to be too narrow to admit the State Coach and was eventually set up outside the Palace in 1828. It was removed to its present site at the north-east corner of Hyde Park in 1851. But once again traffic rendered it useless. It is now on an island site,  housing a small police office which keeps a friendly eye on Speakers' Corner opposite, where Englishmen—and others—can exercise their genius for free speech for the edification, enlightenment and amusement of a crowd which enjoys argument and which is master of the arts of barracking and repartee.

Marble Hill House and Park, at Twickenham. The house is a small but charming example of Palladian architecture beautifully and lovingly restored both without and within by the architects of the Greater London Council. It was designed by Lord Pembroke and Roger Morris in the late 1720s and has a romantic history—it was first occupied by Henrietta Howard, the mistress of George II, and later by Mrs. Fitzherbert, who was secretly married to the Prince Regent (later George IV). Alexander Pope had a hand in the laying out of the grounds. To the student of the best eighteenth-century architecture Marble Hill is a 'must'.

Marlborough House was originally designed by Wren in 1709–10. It was commissioned by the first Duke of Marlborough for his Duchess, the redoubtable Sarah. Its proportions have been spoilt by extra storeys added since. In 1850 it became the official residence of the Prince of Wales, and was the last home of the late Queen Mary. The house has now been converted into a Commonwealth Centre and when not in official use it is open to the public. The Queen's Chapel (p. 90) in the grounds is also shown.

Maundy Money. Maundy Thursday is the day before Good Friday, and the distribution of Maundy Money keeps alive an age-old custom. The earliest reference to the ceremony is in 1300, when the Abbot of Westminster washed the feet of thirteen poor men and afterwards gave them money, food and drink in memory of Christ's washing of His disciples' feet. 'Maundy' is a corruption of the old French and Latin words which also give the modern word 'command'—the Abbot carried out Christ's command. Nowadays the Royal Almoner and his assistants (still carrying towels) assist the monarch or her deputy in the distribution of specially minted Maundy Money in white leather purses. The ceremony takes place every other year in the sanctuary of Westminster Abbey and the principals, carrying nosegays of sweet herbs, are guarded by the Queen's Bodyguard of Yeomen of the Guard.

Mermaid Theatre is built on the site of a bombed warehouse at Puddle Dock, Blackfriars. It is an 'intimate' theatre inspired by the actor-producer Sir Bernard Miles to revive our Elizabethan traditions. Architecturally the structure is a fascinating marriage of modern concrete barrel-vaulting (to give an unrestricted view of the stage from every seat) with much of the brick and cast-iron of the Victorian buildings once on the site. Present plans for enlargement involve building the new 'shell' round it, so productions can continue in it as it is until the last moment.

Middlesex Guildhall stands on the site of the old belfry of Westminster Abbey. Fugitives sought privilege of sanctuary here, and the neighbouring street names of Broad Sanctuary and Little Sanctuary perpetuate the memory of this ancient right. The present building was opened in 1913 and has six court rooms to accommodate the Middlesex Crown Court. During the Second World War these court rooms housed the military and maritime courts of foreign allied powers, and illuminated panels in the entrance hall, signed by the late King George of Greece, Queen Wilhelmina of the Netherlands and King Haakon of Norway, commemorate the fact.

Mint—more correctly the Royal Mint—is on Tower Hill and was partly designed by Sir Robert Smirke in the early nineteenth century. Here are made the coins of the realm, most of the medals of the realm and the State Seals of England. A new Mint has been opened in South Wales, and the London one is closing.

Mitcham Common is large and airy—it provides a public golf course, a boating and swimming pond, and plenty of room for cricket and football. The celebrated Mitcham Fair is held on the north corner of the Common in mid-August.

Monument, in Fish Street Hill, is a hollow fluted column

of Portland stone, surmounted by a platform and a gilded flaming urn. It commemorates the Great Fire of 1666. It is 202 feet high, and is placed exactly 202 feet from the origin of the fire in a baker's shop in Pudding Lane. It has been attributed to Wren but was probably designed by Robert Hooke and was erected in 1671–7. The view from the gallery at the top is well worth the effort of climbing the 311 steps inside the pillar.

Morden College, at Blackheath, is not a college of learning but a residential home for City merchants and members of the learned professions who have fallen on bad times. It was established by a generous City merchant, Sir John Morden, in 1695. It contains some good Lely portraits, an excellent library, a charming chapel with reputed Grinling Gibbons carving, and is set in beautiful well-kept grounds.

Morley College, in Westminster Bridge Road, was born in the dressing rooms of the Old Vic (p. 74). The Vic was originally a Victorian music hall of ill repute and the vision of Emma Cons and the patronage of Samuel Morley combined to transform it into our most serious theatre and a College nearby which is unique. Morley is an evening university for adults of all ages. It is devoted to education for education's sake and especially in the field of music has earned international fame. The College was badly bombed, but a distinguished new building has risen from the ruins and is now open; it displays four new murals—by Edward Bawden, R.A., Martin Froy, John Piper and Justin Todd—which ought to be seen.

Museum for Historical Instruments is housed in the Royal College of Music, Kensington. It has the celebrated Donaldson Collection of over 300 musical instruments of all kinds and ages, including Handel's spinet and Haydn's clavichord, and also the guitar of Rizzio who was music master to Mary Queen of Scots.

N

National Army Museum is housed in a spectacular but restrained modern block designed by Sir William Holford and opened in 1971. It is next door to Wren's Royal Hospital in Chelsea, and they make worthy neighbours. Its historic (and valuable) treasures illustrate the story of the Army from 1485 to 1914. It is London's first, and excellent, twentieth-century museum piece.

National Film Theatre is under the southern arch of Waterloo Bridge. It was inspired by the Telekinema erected nearby for the Festival of Britain and brilliantly solves many problems of sight and sound. It is managed by the British Film Institute and although small is making a great contribution to the art of the cinema.

National Gallery, in Trafalgar Square, was built in 1838 to the curious designs of Wilkins—it was rudely known

as 'the National Cruet Stand' when first erected. From its portico is a fine view of Trafalgar Square and Whitehall with Big Ben, the Victoria Tower and the Vickers building in the distance. Inside is one of the world's finest collections of paintings of all schools. The visitor is recommended to choose the artist, the period, or the school he most favours and to confine his visit to this alone, otherwise his only reward will be a headache and tired feet The attendants are very helpful and lectures under the guidance of experts are given regularly. Standing in front of the west wing is one of London's few worthwhile public memorials—the bronze statue of James II as a Roman emperor by Grinling Gibbons (1686).

National Maritime Museum is in Greenwich, and is centred on the Queen's House (p. 81) in Greenwich Park. It is a permanent record of British seafaring men and their ships, and has a collection of ships' models of all periods and ships' figureheads to delight both young and old. The Nelson gallery has many fascinating relics of the great admiral, including the uniform in which he met his death at Trafalgar. The print room, the library, and the nautical instruments and charts are of special interest to students of maritime history. The Navigation room tells the story of the discovery of longitude, and has Harrison's original chronometer, the first-ever timekeeper accurate enough to be used for navigation, and his three subsequent improved versions. The museum deserves to be known as an art gallery—it includes seascapes by the Van de Veldes, Turner and Muirhead Bone, and the portraits of naval heroes include works by Kneller, Lely, Hogarth, Reynolds, Gainsborough and Romney. The New Neptune Hall presents the story of the boat from pre-history to today and includes the paddle-tug *Reliant*, the world's largest 'ship-in-a-bottle'.

National Portrait Gallery, at the rear of the National Gallery, is primarily an historical record of people who have contributed to the history, and sometimes to the well-being, of the nation. The portraits are chosen more for the fame of their subjects than for their merits as works of art. Nevertheless many great artists are represented, including Holbein, Van Dyck Lely,

Kneller, Hogarth, Romney, Gainsborough, Reynolds and Sargent. The enterprising administration is constantly introducing new ideas and display techniques.

National Postal Museum, in King Edward Street, near St. Paul's, is a comprehensive collection of some 350,000 stamps and other items of interest to postal historians and philatelists of all ages. The recently enlarged museum includes the Reginald M. Phillips collection of nineteenth-century British stamps and the Post Office collections of British and foreign stamps. See also p. 79.

Natural History Museum, more correctly, the British Museum (Natural History), in Cromwell Road, deals with past and existing animal and plant life, and the crust of the earth in relation to life and fossil remains. The building was designed by Alfred Waterhouse and opened in 1881. The Dinosaur Gallery shows immense models and actual fossilized skeletons of many prehistoric monsters, reptiles and birds. The Whale Room

has a full-size cast of a 90-foot-long blue whale. There is a fine specimen of an African elephant in the main hall, and a comprehensive collection of birds and their eggs from all countries. The splendid new Meteorite Pavilion has actual specimens (one weighs $3\frac{1}{2}$ tons), amid speculation and fact about extraterrestrial objects from early Egypt to the latest controversy over tektites. The museum's research work is important—its reference library is one of the finest in the world.

New Zealand House is the London office of the Government of New Zealand and one of London's best post-war buildings. Its fifteen-storey tower on a four-storey base dominates effortlessly and without bombast the junction of Haymarket and Pall Mall.

Old Bailey is the street which has given its name to London's Central Criminal Court, which dominates its northern end. The 1907 building (now with major extensions built on) is pretentious and heavy in detail, but the dome is graceful and very similar, on a smaller scale, to the neighbouring dome of St. Paul's. The bronze statue on the top is by F. W. Pomeroy, and holds a sword aloft in one hand and the scales of justice in the other—it is *not* blindfolded. Here the citizen and the visitor can see British justice in action whenever the courts are sitting. On certain days between May and September the judges carry bouquets of flowers, and sweet herbs are strewn round the courts—a pleasant survival from the days when the judges needed protection from the noxious smells of the old Newgate Prison on whose site the present courts now stand.

Old Curiosity Shop is an antique and gift shop in Portsmouth Street behind the Royalty Theatre in Kingsway. Its association with Dickens's novel has no warrant, but the house dates from the late sixteenth century and is worthy of inspection—it was probably a dairy on the estate which Charles II presented to his Duchess of Portsmouth when cattle grazed in the surrounding fields.

Old Vic. There was a theatre on the site of the present Old Vic in the Waterloo Road in 1818, and in 1833 its name was changed to the Royal Victoria Hall in honour of the Princess Victoria—hence its present name. At the end of the nineteenth century Lilian Baylis became its manageress, and in 1914 her famous Shakespearean company was formed. Opera shared the bill with drama until

Miss Baylis took over the rebuilt Sadler's Wells Theatre (p. 86), and, later, ballet was also presented. The Old Vic suffered badly from bomb damage and was reopened in 1950. It is a temporary home for the National Theatre.

Olympia, at Hammersmith, was first built in 1886, but has been much extended since. The architect of the original Great Hall was H. E. Cole. The new front was added by Joseph Emberton in 1930 and is in grim functional concrete. It is the home of many great exhibitions, including the Ideal Home and Cruft's Dog Show.

Open-Air Music. Sightseeing in London can be hard on the feet. For music-lovers, a rest in the London parks can be especially pleasant during the summer months, listening to military and brass bands from a vantage-point amid the flowers. Usually the music comes free to all who care to pause and listen, and seated comfort for the price of a deck-chair. Arrangements vary from year to year, but good bets for brass band music are usually St. James's Park, Hyde Park and Regent's Park, and Lincoln's Inn Fields some lunch-times, and for light music generally Battersea Park Concert Pavilion, Parliament Hill, Brockwell Park and Clapham Common.

Special sessions at Battersea Park Pavilion cater for jazz fans. They are usually held throughout June and July. The admission charge is moderate. If you prefer your jazz at a distance, stand well back and listen for nothing.

Open-air pop concerts may spring up anywhere. One place is Crystal Palace, where they usually know quite far in advance—telephone 01-778 4691. You can usually learn about others by telephoning 01-229 8219.

One of the most popular London open-air musical treats is the Lakeside Concert season at Kenwood. Saturday evening performances by first-class orchestras take place in Kenwood's concert bowl, mirrored by the lake. Other lakeside concerts are held in the grounds of Crystal Palace, usually for a four-week season from the end of June. Deckchair seats for these concerts, and others at Holland Park, cost about 50p—in advance from the Greater London Council Parks Department, Cavell House, off Trafalgar Square (tel. 01-836 9882) or at the gate on the evening (when you can also get in to sit on the grass for about 30p). Performances naturally depend upon the weather.

Osterley Park is a little to the north of the Great West Road's suburbia. The house was originally built in 1579 for Sir Thomas Gresham, who founded the Royal Exchange (p. 83), but in 1711 it was bought by Francis Child, the banker. In 1761 his grandson, Francis, commissioned Robert Adam to reconstruct the house exactly as Adam wished. The work took fifteen years and, today, Osterley is a precious monument to the genius of Robert Adam. He designed the architectural changes, he designed the furntiure, the carpets, the

ceilings, and every detail of the new interiors, and his beautiful drawings can be seen today alongside their realization. The house and part of the park were presented to the nation by the Earl of Jersey in 1949, and are administered by the Victoria and Albert Museum. The park has much fine woodland, with several lakes, and the stables and out-buildings are nearly as interesting as the house itself.

Oval is the appropriate name given to the ground of the Surrey County Cricket Club. It was first established as a cricket ground in 1845, and is normally used and revered as the site of the final Test Match when Test teams visit England.

P

Pall Mall derives its name from the old game of 'paille-maille' at which Charles II is said to have excelled, and which was played in St. James's Park. The game only survives in the garden of the Freemasons' Arms on the south-western edge of Hampstead Heath. Pall Mall is the High Street of London's clubland (p. 21), linking Trafalgar Square with St. James's Palace.

Parliament Square was originally laid out by Sir Charles Barry to set off his new Houses of Parliament. The Square was brilliantly re-laid by the Ministry of Works in time for the 1951 Festival of Britain—the statues of former statesmen now range the west and north sides, where a raised flower walk gives a perfect view over a wide lawn to the Abbey and Palace of Westminster.

Percival David Foundation of Chinese Art is at 53 Gordon Square, Bloomsbury. This famous collection covers a thousand years of Chinese ceramics and includes the celebrated 'Kitchener Dream Bowl' of the Ming period and an unrivalled assembly of the best examples of the Ch'eng-hua period. There is an excellent reference library on Far Eastern art and culture.

Piccadilly Circus derives its name from 'pickadille', a type of neckwear popular in the eighteenth century. A tailor built a house among a few mansions in what is now Great Windmill Street, and his neighbours promptly dubbed it 'Pickadille Hall' as a reminder to the owner of the source of his wealth. The 'circus' began

to take shape in the late nineteenth century. 'Eros' took up his perch in 1893. It is the work, cast in aluminium, of Sir Alfred Gilbert, and is part of the memorial fountain to the seventh Lord Shaftesbury who was one of our greatest philanthropists. 'Eros' is a misnomer; Gilbert intended his figure to represent The Angel of Christian Charity. Piccadilly Circus is at the heart of the entertainment world of the West End, and its huge neon advertisements are an object of evening pilgrimage for every visitor to London.

Pitshanger Manor is now the Ealing Central Library. The house (1770) was bought by Sir John Soane in 1801 and rebuilt in his own grandiose style. He used Pitshanger as a 'rehearsal' for many of the features he later developed in his celebrated town house (p. 96) in Lincoln's Inn Fields.

Planetarium, next to Mme Tussaud's waxworks (p. 112), is a popular instructional entertainment. Its copper dome on a functional concrete base is a lively addition to a dull main street, and, inside, the mysteries of the heavens are explained by projection from an ingenious and complicated Zeiss instrument and by understandable commentary.

Pollock's Toy Museum, near Goodge Street, is a brave attempt to restore the toy theatre to the popularity it enjoyed throughout most of the last century. Robert Louis Stevenson, a lover of the toy theatre from childhood, in his brilliant essay 'Penny Plain and Twopence Coloured', says 'If you love art, folly, or the bright eyes of children, speed to Pollock's'. There is also a good collection of bygone toys, beautifully dressed dolls from the Continent and the Far East and an excellent display of ingenious early attempts at making moving pictures. An additional delight for the children is the tea-bar, which specializes in another almost forgotten treat, gingerbreads.

Polytechnic, in Upper Regent Street, was founded by Quintin Hogg in 1882. The main building of what is now the Polytechnic of Central London dates from 1911. The Polytechnic was designed to provide for 'the physical, intellectual, social and spiritual needs of youth'. Its activities nowadays cover every field of youthful and adult education and welfare, and its example has been widely copied and extended elsewhere.

Postmen's Park. In a peaceful and leafy oasis, with a tinkling fountain, which was once the churchyard of St. Botolph, Aldersgate (which is hard by), is a modest arcade erected by G. F. Watts in 1887. Its rear wall has a series of plaques which commemorate humble acts of heroism which are otherwise unrecorded. It is a charming idea which is also a fitting memorial to one who, if no great artist, was certainly a distinguished and kindly Victorian.

Post Office Corporation is a general title covering a number of very large buildings from which the complicated postal system of Great Britain is administered. To the public, the Post Office is the King Edward Building near St. Paul's station, where parties by appointment can see not only the sorting of letters but also the unique Post Office Underground Railway and a portion of the City's old walls. The railway is electric and driverless, running underground from Whitechapel Road to Paddington, via Liverpool Street, the King Edward Building and Mount Pleasant, and carrying letters and parcels at a speed of 35 miles an hour with 40 trains an hour in the rush hours. Other branches of the Post Office of interest are the Central Telegraph Office in the Fleet Building, the Faraday Building in Queen Victoria Street, the International Radio Exchange off Cheapside, and Electra House on the Victoria Embankment. The statue of Sir Rowland Hill who introduced the universal penny post to England in 1840 stands outside the King Edward Building. See also National Postal Museum (p. 73).

Post Office Tower, Howland Street, W.1, is London's tallest building. Its primary purpose is to provide a path for telecommunications unimpeded by London's new high buildings. A superb observation platform (temporarily closed) almost 600 ft above ground level gives the visitor a true bird's eye view of the whole of the London basin, and, if he can afford it, there is a slowly revolving restaurant to add a novelty thrill to good food.

Prince Henry's Room, at 17 Fleet Street, dates from 1610. It is on the first floor and was probably the Council Chamber of the Duchy of Cornwall under Henry, the elder son of James I, who died while still Prince of Wales. The plaster ceiling and the carved oak panelling are certainly Jacobean.

Public Record Office, in Chancery Lane, contains the national archives. There is also a small public museum rich in fascinating possessions. Here are the two volumes of William the Conqueror's Domesday Book with a replica which you can handle to see if your native village goes back as far as 1086. Here, too, are examples of Caxton's earliest printing, the first signature of an English King (Richard II), the signatures of Shakespeare and Guy Fawkes, the mediaeval tally system of tax-gathering illustrated by actual split tallies, the log of Nelson's *Victory* at Trafalgar, and Wellington's despatches from Waterloo. There are also historic wills, including those of Shakespeare, Dr. Johnson, Handel, Nelson, Wellington and William Penn. This museum is easily digested and its free fare beyond price.

Queen Anne's Gate is one of the most handsome old streets of London. It is best approached from St. James's Park Underground station. Many of the houses, with elegant doorways, fanlights and carved wooden canopies, date from Queen Anne's time. At No. 26 there is still a torch extinguisher and outside No. 13 is a contemporary statue of Queen Anne—it was carved for the portico of St. Mary-le-Strand Church but never erected there. Students of urban architecture should see and admire Queen Anne's Gate.

The Queen's Gallery is in Buckingham Palace and is reached by a special entry from Buckingham Palace Road. It presents special exhibitions drawn from the vast art collections of the British crown. There is only room for about 30 paintings, a few pieces of furniture and some small drawings, but each exhibition is a chance to inspect rarely seen treasures.

Queen's House is a magnificent jewel set in Greenwich Park and is now a part of the National Maritime Museum (p. 72). It is a very significant house—the forerunner of many 'stately homes'. It was James I who first commissioned Inigo Jones to build at Greenwich a house fit for his queen, Anne of Denmark. In 1619 Anne died and James abandoned the project. In 1629 Charles I ordered Inigo Jones to complete the building in honour of his queen, Henrietta Maria. The result is a masterpiece in the Palladian style which Inigo Jones first introduced to England. Its symmetrical proportions, its perfection of detail and the craftsmanship of marble flooring, wrought-iron balustrading, and carved and painted ceilings, compose a model very rarely equalled in the many great houses which this Queen's House inspired. Amongst many pictures is a fine portrait of Inigo Jones by Hogarth.

R

Regent's Park was once a royal hunting ground. It was laid out by Nash as a park for a house which the Prince Regent planned to build on Primrose Hill. The park was opened to the public in 1838. The southern portion of the Outer Circle is terraced with fine stucco houses by John Nash and Decimus Burton. This is London's most complete park—it has everything a park ought to have. There is a yachting and boating lake for adults, a boating pond for children, a magnificent rose and rock garden (Queen Mary's Gardens), shady avenues of chestnuts and elms, wide playing fields, tennis courts, an open-air theatre, and on its northern side the famous enclosures of the Zoological Society (p. 124). The flowers, the trees, the shrubs and the lawns of Regent's Park are worth a visit at any time of the year. By the lake is Bedford College founded for women in 1849 (in Bedford Square) and now part of the University of London.

Richmond Park, Surrey, is the largest urban park in Britain and is near enough and old enough to bring the authentic rural air to town. It was first enclosed by Charles I as a deer park, and large herds of fallow and of red deer still roam there. The park is well wooded with majestic oaks and rhododendron plantations, and Pen Ponds in the centre are a perfect sanctuary for water fowl and a great rendezvous for ice skaters in winter. **White Lodge,** near Roehampton Gate, was built by George II as a hunting box; it was the birthplace of the Duke of Windsor and, for a time, the late King George VI lived there when he was Duke of York. It is now the home of the Royal Ballet School. On Richmond Green is the old gateway to Henry VII's **Richmond Palace,** and from the Terrace Gardens on Richmond Hill is the magnificent view of the Thames Valley immortalized by Turner. There are two public golf courses on the Roehampton side of the park. On the south-west side, beautiful walks lead down to the riverside commons of Ham (p. 43) and Petersham.

Roman Bath, at 5 Strand Lane, is an antiquarian's mystery, and no reputable authority will vouch for its Latinity. But it is an interesting relic. The oval lead overflow pipe is considered to be genuinely Roman but the bricks are more probably Tudor.

Royal Academy was founded in 1768 under royal patronage 'for promoting the arts of design', but it was not until a century later that it went to its present home at Burlington House in Piccadilly. The title of Royal Academician is awarded to forty members who at 75 years of age become Senior Academicians leaving vacancies for Royal Academicians; the title of Associate is limited to thirty from whom vacancies for the full membership are filled. The R.A.'s Summer Exhibition, from May till August, has been held regularly since 1769, and gives all British artists the opportunity of recognition and of display without commission charges

—provided their work is accepted by the selection panel. Competition is severe—on the average only 1,500 works can be shown out of a total of about 11,000 submitted. During most of the rest of the year, special exhibitions from collections at home and abroad are usually arranged. Burlington House also includes the Royal Academy Schools (which have trained many of our most famous artists, including Lawrence, Turner, Constable and Millais) and is the headquarters of several learned societies.

Royal Exchange, in Cornhill, dates from 1844 and is the third Royal Exchange—the first was founded by Elizabethan Sir Thomas Gresham in 1564 and destroyed in the Great Fire of 1666; the second was burnt in 1838. The present pavement of Turkey stone belonged to the first building. New sovereigns are always proclaimed from the steps leading up to the Corinthian portico. Inside is a covered quadrangle used for business up to 1939, and surrounded by frescoes depicting London's history. The statue of Queen Victoria in the middle of the quadrangle is by Sir Hamo Thornycroft, and in front of the Exchange is an equestrian statue of the Duke of Wellington, riding without stirrups, by Chantrey (1844), and a war memorial to London troops by Alfred Drury (1920).

Royal Festival Hall was born of the decision to hold the main London section of the 1951 Festival of Britain on

the derelict South Bank site, and the L.C.C.'s resolve to complete a long cherished project for a cultural centre in a place of past squalor. The result is a Concert Hall which such great conductors as Toscanini have declared the finest in the world. The amenities, the planning and the décor of the interior have received almost universal praise. The designers were Robert Matthew and J. L. Martin.

Royal Geographical Society was founded in 1830 and now occupies Lowther Lodge in Kensington Gore, an interesting example of the town architecture of Norman Shaw (1874). There is a small museum.

Royal Institute of British Architects (founded 1834) in Portland Place has an interesting building designed by Grey Wornum. The exterior, with the sculptures on the main entrance pylons by James Woodford and reliefs by Bainbridge Copnall, has not received the same unqualified praise as the interior lecture hall, library, and council room The Institute's vast collection of architectural drawings is now housed at the charming Heinz Gallery at 21 Portman Square, where small but choice periodic exhibitions are open to the public on weekday afternoons.

Royal Mews is in Buckingham Palace Road behind Buckingham Palace. Here the royal coaches and horses used on state occasions are usually stabled. These include the State Coach designed for George III and used for coronations, the Irish State Coach bought by Queen

Victoria in 1852 and used for state openings of Parliament, the Glass State Coach bought by George V in 1910 and now used for royal weddings, and several state landaus and carriages for great royal events. The State Coach harness is considered the finest in the world.

Royal Naval College dominates the river front of Greenwich—it is built on the site of the old Greenwich Palace of Placentia. It was begun under William and Mary and completed in 1752 as a Royal Hospital for disabled seamen, and became the Royal Naval College for the training of officers in 1873. The Painted Hall was designed by Wren and was completed in 1703. The ceiling and wall panels are by Sir James Thornhill. The chapel was completed in 1752 from the designs of Wren. These were modified after a fire in 1779 and the chapel restored in an ornate Greek style by James Stuart. The circular pulpit, the lectern and the font, all of wood, were carved in the old naval dockyards at Deptford.

Royal Observatory, in Greenwich Park, was founded by Charles II in 1675 primarily to assist navigation. In 1950 most of the work of the observatory was transferred to Herstmonceux Castle in Sussex where the air is clearer. But the Octagon Room of **Flamsteed House** remains very much as its architect Wren left it. The house is now an extension of the National Maritime Museum (p. 72) dealing with astronomy and navigation. A mast on the east turret carries the famous time ball which falls precisely at 13 00 daily. Leading from the Observatory enclosure across a path in Greenwich Park is the brass strip which marks the meridian, and those who stand astride it can truly say they are standing in both the eastern and western hemispheres. Near the observatory is a statue of General Wolfe by the Canadian sculptor Tait Mackenzie (1930). Wolfe's tomb is in the crypt of the nearby parish church of St. Alfege built by Wren's pupil Hawksmoor in 1718. The view from Observatory Hill provides a splendid panorama with Greenwich Park and all its noble buildings in the foreground and the river beyond.

Royal Society of Arts, in John Adam Street, Strand, was founded in 1754 'for the advancement, development and application of every department of Science in connection with Arts, Manufactures and Commerce'. At first its work was mostly concerned with agriculture—it introduced the swede and mangel-wurzel into this country— but with the coming of the Industrial Revolution its scope widened to include the whole field of industrial design. The Great Exhibition of 1851 was one of its most spectacular achievements. Today, its influence is largely maintained through its distinguished lecturers. The beautiful headquarters building was designed for the R.S.A. by the brothers Adam in 1774 and is a perfect specimen of their work. It is one of the few buildings remaining of the famous Adelphi scheme, now sacrificed to the grandiose ugliness of modern business.

R.W.S. Galleries, in Conduit Street, are the home of the Royal Society of Painters in Water Colours, which was founded in 1804.

Sadler's Wells. In 1683, workmen excavating in the garden of one Thomas Sadler's house in Islington unearthed an ancient well which rapidly became a popular spa. The life of Sadler's Wells as a theatre began when Sadler built a small theatre out of his original house as an additional attraction to the well. In 1931 this was completely rebuilt and became, under the management of Lilian Baylis, a national home of opera in English. In August 1968 the Opera Company moved to a more spacious home at the Coliseum Theatre, St. Martin's Lane, and the Theatre now accommodates all kinds of visiting companies.

St. Aidan's Roman Catholic Church, East Acton, coolly modern in manner, if architecturally unadventurous, has, however, a particular title to fame. Above the altar is a magnificent *Crucifixion* specially painted for St. Aidan's by Graham Sutherland. Of infinite compassion and majesty, it is an outstanding example of the work of a great living British painter.

St. Albans, in Hertfordshire, was a Roman city for 400 years. St. Alban was a Roman soldier serving in the garrison of Verulamium, who became Britain's first Christian martyr in the early fourth century. St. Albans became an important mediaeval city which finally won its freedom from thraldom to the great Abbey of St. Albans in whose famous scriptorium so many of our mediaeval chronicles were inscribed. The modern town has much good eighteenth-century brick, a fine centre in St. Peter's Street, and the ancient church of St. Michael where Francis Bacon was buried. But visitors will rightly give most of their attention to the Verulamium Museum, the Roman hypocaust, the Roman theatre, the Roman wall, and, of course, to the cathedral.

St. Albans Cathedral was a Norman abbey church, which only became a cathedral in 1877. The tower and main transept walls reveal its history—they are made of local stone and flints and many Roman tiles and bricks taken from the site of Verulamium. The interior has been much restored, but the Norman proportions remain and some excellent mediaeval wall paintings have been revealed. Apart from the Great Gateway, now part of St. Albans School, little else remains of the large mediaeval abbey.

St. Bartholomew the Great, in Smithfield, is the City's oldest and most interesting church. It is all that remains

of the Priory of St. Bartholomew founded in 1123 by
the monk Rahere who also founded London's first hospital over the way. At the Reformation, the Priory nave
was demolished and the original choir became a parish
church—it is a magnificent example of apsidal Norman
architecture. The church has many interesting relics
including the effigy and tomb of Rahere, and its half-
timbered Tudor Gatehouse (1595) looks out on ground
rich in history (see page 97).

St. Bride's is the parish church of Fleet Street, with a
long history of service to printers and journalists. This
began in 1500 when Wynkyn de Worde set up his
printing press 'in Fletestrete at the signe of the Swane'.
But the church is in fact much older, for this is the
eighth church on the site. The foundations of the
previous seven were excavated before the church was
rebuilt after wartime destruction. Only its amusing
Wren wedding-cake steeple survived the bombing, but
the church has been splendidly restored since in the
Wren manner. In the crypt a small but fascinating
museum tells the story of the site from Roman times.

St. Clement Danes is one of the two 'island' churches in
the Strand; it was badly damaged by bombing. The
Wren fabric (1681) was a mere shell, but the tower by
James Gibbs (1719) survived intact. The church is now
fully restored as the church of the Royal Air Force, and
has two claims to fame. It is the church of the 'Oranges
and Lemons' nursery rhyme, and every March a special
children's service is held when each child on leaving
is presented with an orange and a lemon. It was also
the church of Dr. Johnson, and his statue outside the
east end is an appropriate memorial facing the Doctor's
beloved Fleet Street. As St. Clement is a patron saint
of seamen, the church's weather-vane incorporates an
anchor and the vicarage is known as the Anchorage.
The reason for 'Danes' is hard to find, although the
tradition is that on this site were once a Danish settle-
ment and the burial place of Harold Harefoot.

St. Etheldreda's Church, in Ely Place (p. 31), is the only pre-Reformation church in London which has been restored to Roman Catholic authority. It was originally the chapel of the Bishops of Ely whose palace was in Ely Place, and dates from the late thirteenth century. The most interesting surviving part of the church is the original crypt in which there are traces of an even earlier building.

St. George's Church, Hanover Square, was built in 1713–24 by John James, a pupil of Wren. The three east windows are of Flemish glass of the early sixteenth century representing a Tree of Jesse. The church is well known for its fashionable weddings—here Sir William Hamilton, Shelley, Disraeli, 'George Eliot' and Theodore Roosevelt were married.

St. James's Church, Piccadilly, is the only West End church designed by Wren (1684). It has a reredos and an organ case, and also a less-distinguished marble font, all authentically by Grinling Gibbons. The church suffered heavily from bombing but has been well restored. The churchyard is a peaceful oasis amid the roar of Piccadilly.

St. James's Palace, at the bottom of St. James's Street, off Piccadilly, is a rather mutilated but still romantic

example of Tudor brick-work. It was named from the Norman leper hospital (dedicated to St. James the Less, Bishop of Jerusalem) which was demolished by Henry VIII to make room for a palace. Until Buckingham Palace succeeded it, St. James's was the London home of successive sovereigns—which accounts for the fact that ambassadors to this country are still accredited 'to the Court of St. James'. Other members of the royal family still reside within its precincts. There are two Chapels Royal attached to the palace. Off Ambassadors Court is the chapel of the original building (1532) with a magnificent ceiling attributed to Holbein and certainly by a master-hand. The other chapel is in Marlborough Road and is known as the Queen's Chapel because it was designed by Inigo Jones for Henrietta Maria, the queen of Charles I. The choirboys' dress is scarlet and gold Tudor costume. The chapel itself, with its Carolean panelling, its royal pews, its beautiful proportions and its ornate roof, is an architectural masterpiece too little known. The sentries—usually from the Guards Division in full dress but occasionally from other famous British and Commonwealth regiments—are a popular London sight, and visitors can walk through some of the courtyards—sentries notwithstanding.

St. James's Park, although one of the smaller royal parks, is the prettiest, and the flower beds, trees and shrubberies are superb at any time of year. The park was originally a swampy field until it was drained and made into a pleasure ground and a nursery for deer by Henry VIII. It was later re-modelled by Nash. The

islands of the lake are bird sanctuaries, and children and office workers as well as politicians and ornithologists take pleasure in feeding the many varieties of duck and wild fowl, and in trying to tempt the comical pelicans from their island homes. There are plenty of deck chairs for the visitor who is weary of sightseeing. Overlooking the park from the north are the two stucco blocks of **Carlton House Terrace,** the final link in the chain of Nash's work from Regent's Park southwards.

St. James's Square was originally planned in the time of Charles II as an exclusive residential quarter. Chatham House (No. 10), on the north side, was the residence of three Prime Ministers—William Pitt, Earl of Chatham, the Earl of Derby and W. E. Gladstone. The original torch extinguishers are still fitted to the obelisks on either side of the steps of the house, which is now the headquarters of the Royal Institute of International Affairs. Robert Walpole, the Earl of Chesterfield, and Josiah Wedgwood are other distinguished names associated with the Square, and Norfolk House on the south-east corner was used by Eisenhower for the planning of the invasions of North Africa and Europe. In the north-west corner is the London Library—England's most famous subscription library founded by Carlyle and first opened in 1841. It now possesses half-a-million volumes. In the well-laid-out gardens of the square is an equestrian statue erected in 1808 of William of Orange by John Bacon the younger. Under the horse's hooves is the molehill it tripped on, causing William's death.

St. John's Church, Clerkenwell, just north of Smithfield, was the Priory Church of the Order of St. John of Jerusalem. It was gutted in the war, but is now fully restored. It contains the side panels of a fifteenth-century Flemish triptych. The crypt remained undamaged—the main nave is pure Norman, the side chapels are Early English Gothic. It has now been converted into two chapels.

St. John's Gate, in Clerkenwell, was the main entrance to the ancient Priory of the Order of St. John. The Priory was destroyed at the Dissolution, but in 1831 the Order was revived as a benevolent institution closely associated with ambulance and hospital work. The Gate dates from 1504, with parts from much earlier days, and the rooms over it are now used as the headquarters of the Order. They contain many interesting relics of the Order which was originally founded in the time of King Stephen (1135–54) as the crusading Order of the Knights Hospitallers of St. John of Jerusalem.

St. Margaret's Church, Westminster, in Parliament Square, is a twelfth-century foundation, but the present church dates from 1523. Since 1614 it has been the official church of the House of Commons. The east window is our best example of fifteenth-century Flemish glass—it was a gift from Ferdinand and Isabella of Spain to Henry VII for his chapel in Westminster Abbey on the betrothal of Prince Arthur to their daughter Katharine of Aragon. By the time the glass arrived Henry VIII was king and had married his brother's widow. The glass was sent to Waltham Abbey and was transferred to St. Margaret's in 1758. Raleigh and Hollar were buried in the church, and Caxton was buried in the churchyard. Today the church is chiefly known for its fashionable weddings, but its Elizabethan and Jacobean monuments are excellent.

St. Martin-in-the-Fields Church, in Trafalgar Square, is fully entitled 'the Royal Parish Church of St. Martin-in-the-Fields' and carries the royal arms over the porch. It was built in 1726 by James Gibbs, a pupil of Wren. The interior has a beautiful elliptical fretted ceiling of Italian workmanship, but is otherwise severely classical. The church is the parish church of the Lords Commissioners of the Admiralty and on all state occasions flies the White Ensign. The vaults used to be open each evening to the poor and homeless, and in the early days of broadcasting the church was famous for the sermons of the Rev. Dick Sheppard, a great preacher, a great philanthropist and a founder of the modern pacifist movement.

St. Mary-le-Strand Church, in the Strand, was completed in 1717 to the baroque designs of James Gibbs. Its severe but well-proportioned interior is relieved by a magnificent Italianate ceiling and its rectangular spire is graceful and interesting. The portico was to be crowned with the statue of Queen Anne which is now in Queen Anne's Gate (p. 80).

St. Nicholas's Church, Deptford Green, is the church

most closely associated with the seafaring traditions of
the old Deptford Dockyard. Drake and Hawkins wor-
shipped here. Pepys knew it well. But perhaps the most
interesting of its many associations is the entry in the
Parish records under June 1st 1593 'Christopher
Marlowe, slaine by Francis Friser'. The church suffered
badly from bombing, but the tower (*circa* 1500) remained and many of the memorials were saved—it is
now fully restored. St. Nicholas is a patron saint of
seafarers.

St. Paul's Cathedral is the cathedral church of the diocese
of London and the masterpiece in Portland stone of Sir
Christopher Wren. It was begun in 1675 and completed
in 1710, and Wren's assistants included such distinguished men as Hawksmoor, Tijou, Grinling Gibbons
Cibber and Bird. The pre-
sent cathedral was built
on the site of Old St.
Paul's, the vast and lofty
Gothic masterpiece which
was finally destroyed in
the Great Fire of 1666.

The architectural in-
terest of St. Paul's is that
it is a brilliant marriage
between Gothic structure
and classical Renaissance
presentation. Cruciform
plan, transepts, chancel and aisles, even flying buttresses
are clothed in the décor of early baroque. Its site dominates the City, and the splendid view of the exterior
which bombing revealed from the north east is preserved.
The interior is magnificent (if most of the memorials are
ignored), the choir stalls were carved by Grinling
Gibbons, and the new high altar from a design by Wren
and dedicated to the fallen of the Commonwealth is now
in use. It is guarded by Tijou's magnificent screens.
Behind it is the American Memorial Chapel. Visitors
should certainly climb to the Whispering Gallery round

the inside of the dome—not only to hear the whispers but to appreciate the size and proportions of the central space below. The exterior Stone Gallery and Golden Gallery give splendid views of the whole of London.

There are three memorials which are worth special study—the inscription on the wall of the crypt above the tomb of Sir Christopher Wren 'Lector, si monumentum requiris, circumspice' (Reader, if you seek a memorial, look about you), Nelson's tomb in the crypt (p. 26) and on the south wall of the choir the effigy of Dr. John Donne the poet, Dean of St. Paul's from 1621 to 1631, which survived the Great Fire.

In the churchyard, where the bronze figure of St. Paul now stands, is the site of Paul's Cross where sermons were preached, Papal Bulls promulgated, ecclesiastical threats and prohibitions announced and royal messages proclaimed in mediaeval days.

Visitors should not miss the eighteenth-century brick Deanery across the road to the south in Dean's Court.

Salisbury Hall, at London Colney in Hertfordshire, is a picturesque mid-seventeenth-century brick and stone mansion built for Sir Jeremy Snow, a courtier of Charles II. It is surrounded by a mediaeval moat. The interior has some good original panelling and two fine fireplaces. Both Charles I and Charles II visited the Hall and Sir Winston Churchill spent part of his boyhood there. The Mosquito aeroplane of the Second World War was designed and built there and the prototype is on show.

Salutes. The firing of salutes in London takes place on such set occasions as royal births, the accession of the sovereign and its anniversaries, the royal family birthdays, the official birthday of the sovereign (normally the first or second Saturday in June) and state openings of Parliament. But special occasions may include such events as the arrival of visiting royalty. A royal salute is normally of 21 guns, but in Hyde Park 41 guns are fired, the extra twenty commemorating the days when private citizens of London owned ordnance and joined in royal salutes. Royal salutes are fired in Hyde Park by The King's Troop, Royal Horse Artillery (p. 59), while salutes at the Tower are the privilege of the Honourable Artillery Company (p. 49). There, a total of 62 guns are fired, the extra ones being in honour of the City.

Savoy Chapel, in Savoy Street, off the Strand, or more fully, the Queen's Chapel of the Savoy, is the private property of the monarch who, as Duke of Lancaster (male or female), inherits the remains of the estate of John of Gaunt, Duke of Lancaster (1340–99). Gaunt's palace on the site was razed to the ground during the Peasants' Revolt of 1381, but much rebuilding took place under Henry VII. When the National Anthem is sung the first two lines of the Chapel version are 'God save our gracious Queen, Long live our noble Duke . . .' The Chapel is the home of the Royal Victorian Order which is the personal Order of the sovereign. The royal pews are at the west end, and tradition says that the picture over the altar was presented by Chaucer who may have been married in the original Chapel.

Science Museum, in Exhibition Road, South Kensington, illustrates the application of science to industry and to our daily lives—it is therefore as interesting to the general public as to the professional scientist. For the schoolboy it is a paradise. Here are Puffing Billy (1813) and Stephenson's Rocket (1829) side by side with models of modern locomotives. Here is the mechanism

 of mine and pump revealed at the press of a button. Here is a visual history of man's conquest of the air, and now in Gallery 66 a magnificent display to elucidate the history of telecommunications. The Children's Gallery, with its dioramic history of the development of transport and power throughout the ages, fascinates parents as much as children.

Scotland Yard. The original Scotland Yard was that part of the old Whitehall Palace used by Scottish kings visiting London—it was at the north end of modern Whitehall. It was not until 1842 that the Metropolitan Police formed a detective force housed in this Scotland Yard. In 1890 they moved to the riverside building by Norman Shaw which was to become world-famous as New Scotland Yard. In 1967 Scotland Yard moved yet again—this time to a towering new block in Broadway, off Victoria Street. It houses the entire headquarters organization of the Metropolitan Police, including the Information Room, which maintains radio contact with all police cars and launches, laboratories, television studios and, of course, the vast Criminal Record Office.

Shell Centre is on the South Bank of the Thames at Waterloo. Whether this functional tower block is an ornament to London's skyline is open to question, but nevertheless its interior is interesting and from its 25th floor (317 ft.) there is a public viewing gallery which puts the whole of London at your feet. The architect was Sir Howard Robertson.

Shows for Youngsters. Special children's shows are given free in some London parks during the summer months. Entertainments include puppet shows and pantomimes. The ruddy face of Mr. Punch can often be seen with Judy and that ever popular success, the crocodile. A telephone call to the local borough council offices or the Greater London Council Parks Department—01-836 5464—will give you dates and times.

Silver Vaults, below street level at 53 Chancery Lane, are fascinating Aladdin's Caves of mostly antique silverware open to the public. It is a paradise for those who love silver, especially if their purses are also silver-lined.

Sir John Soane's Museum, at 13 Lincoln's Inn Fields, was designed for himself by Sir John Soane (1753–1837) both as a home and as a museum to house his astonishing collection of antiquities and paintings. Sir John Soane's chief work was the Bank of England, but his influence was more important than his performance. The house is preserved very much as its designer knew it, except that a Students' Room has replaced his private office. The rooms are crowded with fragments and statuary from all periods, including much from Greece and Italy and the sarcophagus of King Seti I (*circa* 1370 B.C.) of Egypt, and in the Picture Room are two famous series of paintings by William Hogarth—'The Rake's Progress' and 'The Election'. The museum contains over 20,000 architectural drawings. The architectural student and the antiquarian will find the museum's treasures inexhaustible; the ordinary public will enjoy the pictures (which also include works by Turner and Reynolds) and the furniture, and admire the ingenuity with which Soane used mirror-glass.

Smithfield Market. From the early twelfth century the great St. Bartholomew Fair (August 24th) was held at Smithfield—it was our greatest Cloth Fair when England depended for its wealth on the export of wool and cloth. By the fourteenth century its green open space was used as a cattle market and also for archery and tournaments. Here the boy king Richard II faced the peasants in the Revolt of 1381 and saw Wat Tyler slain; and here the Martyrs (both Protestant and Roman Catholic) were burned at the stake in the sixteenth century. A visit to the vast halls of Smithfield's modern meat market in the early hours of the morning before London's meat is distributed is an astonishing experience.

Soho is the foreign-speaking island bounded by Shaftesbury Avenue, Oxford Street and Regent Street. It became the home of Huguenot refugees from France after 1685 and has retained its foreign flavour. For anything but plain English cooking Soho is a worthwhile adventure, and the shops are as fascinating as the inhabitants.

Somerset House was built on the site of the palace begun by the Protector, Duke of Somerset, in 1547, but halted when he was executed in 1552. The present building has its main entrance in the Strand, but its front faces the river, and, before the Victoria Embankment was built, the central arch of the basement arcade was a Water Gate. The south front was built by Sir William Chambers in 1777–86, the east wing (now King's College of London University) by Sir Robert Smirke in 1828–34, and the west wing by Sir James Pennethorne in 1854–6. The Royal Academy, the Royal Society and the Society of Antiquaries, now at Burlington House, were originally at Somerset House. It is now the headquarters of the Board of Inland Revenue, and also the home of the Probate Registry and the Registrar General. The best view of Somerset House is from the terrace on the South Bank looking under the arches of Waterloo Bridge.

South Africa House, on the east side of Trafalgar Square, was designed by Sir Herbert Baker and opened in 1933 as the London headquarters of the South African Government. The exterior of Portland stone on a granite base is of no great distinction, but the interior décor illustrates the resources, beauty and history of South Africa. The gilded winged springbok outside is by Sir Charles Wheeler, and the magnificent tapestry map in the Entrance Hall was designed by Macdonald Gill and woven on the Morris looms of Merton Abbey. There is a library, a reference room and an exhibition hall.

South Bank Arts Centre at present consists of three fine concert halls and an art gallery. Fitting neatly between the formal symmetry of the Royal Festival Hall (p. 84), the oldest of the three halls, and Waterloo Bridge (p. 9), is the new complex containing the Queen Elizabeth Hall, the Purcell Room and the Hayward Gallery (p. 47). Built in unfaced concrete, the buildings are (to some eyes) brutal but undeniably functional. The National Theatre is also to have its home here, adding drama to music and the visual arts.

South Bank Lion was once both a trade mark and a landmark on the Lion Brewery near Hungerford Bridge. For the Festival of Britain in 1951 it was moved to a site outside the main entrance to Waterloo Station. The Lion has now found a permanent home outside County Hall at Westminster Bridge. It is of great interest because it was made in 1837 of Coade stone—an artificial stone from a factory opened in 1769 by Eleanor Coade in Lambeth. The secret of its composition has regrettably been lost—it is incomparably the most long-lasting artificial stone ever invented. The Lion was designed by W. F. Woodington.

South London Art Gallery in Peckham Road, Camberwell, was the first London gallery to be open on Sundays. It owes its inception (1891) to Lord Leighton, G. F. Watts, Frampton and Walter Crane. There are special loan exhibitions from time to time.

Southwark Cathedral, at the southern end of London Bridge, is a restored mediaeval church of great beauty and interest. It has Norman remains, it has a perfect Early English Lady Chapel and an altar screen built in 1520 by that Chancellor Bishop Fox who also embellished his own Cathedral of Winchester and founded the College of Corpus Christi at Oxford. The decorated tomb and effigy  of John Gower (1408), the friend of Chaucer and one of our earliest (and dullest) poets, is in the nave. The Chapel of St. John the Evangelist is now known as the Harvard Chapel, after its restoration by Harvard University in honour of its founder, John Harvard, who was baptized in the church in 1607. Shakespeare's younger brother, who died in the same year, is also buried here.

Sport. The sporting visitor to London has plenty of scope. London's parks will please many, for most of them have bowling greens and tennis courts, and some have putting greens, all for public use at modest charges.

In Hyde Park or Regent's Park, you can cast off and test your seamanship in a sailing dinghy; rowing boats can be hired in almost any park with a big enough stretch of water. In some places (notably Regent's Park) there is a special shallow pool for children's boating.

Before you tackle boating, make sure you can swim. There is a special section on London's swimming pools on p. 104.

Golf is growing in popularity, and if you cannot get an introduction to play on a private course, there are two public courses in Richmond Park, one at Mitcham, and several in such outer suburbs as Beckenham and Hainault. To play on the public course in Epping Forest at Chingford you must wear a red jacket.

Ice skating in the open air depends on the winter but there are indoor ice-rinks at Richmond, Streatham and Bayswater for those whose patience wears as thin as the winter ice. Skiers also do not have to wait on the weather; there are artificial ski-slopes at Crystal Palace and Alexandra Palace where you can learn the easy way. But you will need to book in advance.

Until the Industrial Revolution, the Thames was still a salmon river. Recently fish have been found again near the Pool of London—a tribute to modern sewage disposal techniques. Although it is too early to suggest that the Central London visitor can now have a rewarding day with his rod, the Thames west of London can provide good coarse (and some trout) fishing. The stretch from Hampton Court to Kingston has a reputation for barbel. The reservoirs at Barnes can be fished from mid-June to mid-March on day tickets obtainable from the Metropolitan Water Board. Pike, perch, roach, bream, rudd, dace, tench, gudgeon, eels, chub may all be met in fresh water, and the novice is recommended to find out from his local tackle shop which are likely to be encountered, and the baits that are most likely to be successful. No river authority licence is required to fish in water of the Thames Conservancy Board and the Lee Conservancy Catchment Board. On most parts of the Lee Navigation fishing is free; certain sections are controlled by clubs, day tickets are available to fish in their waters. The Pen Ponds in Richmond Park can be fished (mostly roach and perch) if you obtain a permit from the Superintendent, Richmond Park, and the ponds on Hampstead Heath need no permits.

Staple Inn, in Holborn, was at one time a hostel or centre of the fourteenth-century Wool Staplers, and later became one of the Inns of the Courts of Chancery. Its fine sixteenth-century hall and pretty courtyard—the headquarters of the Institute of Actuaries—were destroyed by a bomb in 1944, but are now fully restored. The picturesque Tudor houses of the Holborn frontage survive. They date from 1586, but were heavily restored in 1937. Dr. Johnson lived in Staple Inn from 1759–60 and is said to have written *Rasselas* there in a week to pay for his mother's funeral.

State Opening of Parliament takes place annually in late October or early November or at the opening of a new parliament after a general election. The public is given a splendid opportunity of demonstrating its loyalty as the sovereign is driven in the Irish State Coach, with a royal escort, from Buckingham Palace via The Mall to the House of Lords. A royal salute is fired from Hyde Park (p. 94).

Stations. Four of London's main line railway termini are of interest as works of architecture in the serivce of transport:

Euston Station has been completely reconstructed in recent years. Instead of Hardwicke's heavy pseudo-classical Victoriana there is now a spacious well-lit concourse in aluminium, glass and concrete, with ramps down to the platforms, and escalators direct to the Underground ticket hall. The Doric arch which once stood at the entrance now survives only in the tiled motifs on the platform walls of the Victoria Line Underground station below.

King's Cross Station was designed by Lewis Cubitt (1851–2) and is an admirable example of functional architecture many years ahead of its time. The clock on the station tower was originally on the Crystal Palace in Hyde Park during the 1851 exhibition. The design may have been broadly based on the Tsar's Riding Stables in Moscow.

Paddington Station is fundamentally the work (1854) of Isambard Kingdom Brunel, the famous engineer of the old G.W.R. The hotel which hides the functional iron and glass of the station proper was designed by the younger Hardwick (1854) in the then newly fashionable French Renaissance style.

St. Pancras Station has a frontage by Sir George Gilbert Scott (1873–6) in a Lombardic and Venetian brick Gothic style. The extravagant romanticism of these buildings should not blind the observer to the functional daring of the glass and iron vault (by Barlow) which covers the platforms behind—it has the unprecedented span of 243 feet and a length of 690 feet.

Stock Exchange, colloquially known as 'the House', is close to the Bank of England. It was first founded in 1801 and in 1970 moved into a new building in Old Broad Street. The public can see (but not hear) the brokers and jobbers in action from a visitors' gallery overlooking 'the floor'.

Strand was really a 'strand' in earlier times—a pleasant walk along the river between the City of London and the Abbey and Palace of Westminster. In Stuart times the Strand was bordered by aristocratic mansions with gardens extending down to the river. The names of some of them survive in Somerset House, and Bedford, Villiers, and Southampton Streets. Until the 1920s there was an amusing sequence of street names on the south side—GEORGE Street, VILLIERS Street, DUKE Street, OF Alley, BUCKINGHAM Street. The Strand of today is full of interest—it has one of our worst station fronts and a Victorian guess at an Eleanor Cross which gave the 'Cross' to the village of Charing, Coutts' Bank (founded 1692) with which the royal family has banked for two centuries, Rhodesia House (closed) with its Epstein sculptures disgracefully mutilated for safety's sake, Shell-Mex House, the Savoy Hotel and Savoy Theatre, where most of the Gilbert and Sullivan operas were first produced, and finally, on the north side, Bush House, Australia House, and the Law Courts. Just off the north side, opposite Charing Cross Station, is the pleasantly proportioned stucco front of Charing Cross Hospital, founded in 1818 and built in 1831 by Decimus Burton. But the Strand is primarily a street to 'go down' —to Nelson on his column (p. 111) or the graceful spire of St. Clement Danes (p. 88).

Strand-on-the-Green is a pretty riverside village near Kew Bridge with only a pathway between the old houses and the water.

Strawberry Hill, at Twickenham, is the fascinating result of Horace Walpole's enthusiasm for Gothic. It is one of our earliest examples of the Gothic Revival. Walpole bought 'a little plaything house' near the river and converted it (1750–76) into a rococo and romantic castle. The house is now occupied by a training college, but permission to see this architectural enterprise is always given to the serious student.

Street Markets. No student of contemporary London should miss sampling at least one of its colourful street markets where the bargain hunters forage to great profit —if they are lucky. The best known markets are Petticoat Lane (Middlesex Street), a general market which

flourishes on Sunday mornings, and Portobello Road, renowned for its antiques. Others worth a visit (check days and times first) include: Walthamstow (now on the Underground), Berwick Market, Club Row (Sclater Street), The Cut, Leather Lane, Caledonian Market, Chapel Market, and Camden Passage.

Swimming. For those who care to brave the English weather (it's often warmer in the water than out) there are some open-air swimming pools to choose from. The Oasis, near Holborn, and the Serpentine Lido in Hyde Park are the most central, but there are also swimming places in the ponds of Hampstead and Highgate; Highgate Pond caters for men only, Kenwood Pond for women, Hampstead Pond at South End Green offers mixed bathing. These are for experienced swimmers; whereas the Parliament Hill Lido at Gospel Oak is excellent for children. The less hardy can swim indoors or enjoy warm bathing all year round at Marshall Street Baths, just off Regent Street. A few minutes out by Underground you can bathe amid typical modern architecture in the Swiss Cottage Baths designed by Sir Basil Spence. Further out, the Rickmansworth Aquadrome and the Lido at Ruislip have facilities for swimming and various water-sports as well. Explorers will discover their own favourites for themselves.

Syon House, at Isleworth, was built on the site of the Bridgettine Convent of 'Syon' founded by Henry v in 1415 and moved to Isleworth in 1431. It is now one of the great houses of the Dukes of Northumberland. The exterior is still more or less as the Protector Somerset knew it. The arcade facing the river is attributed to Inigo Jones, the entrance gateway and most of the interior are by Robert Adam (1761). The grounds, laid out by 'Capability' Brown, are the setting for the Gardening Centre (p. 36). The Great Hall is Adam's masterpiece. The Gallery was described by Adam as 'finished in a style to afford variety and amusement' and he spoke with truth. There are many pictures, including portraits by Lely, Reynolds and Gainsborough. The gardens reaching to the river bank are famous for their rich variety of shrubs and magnificent oaks. The lion on the river front was removed from Northumberland House at Charing Cross when the building was demolished in 1874. Syon House is a monument to the Age of Elegance.

T

Tate Gallery, on the embankment at Millbank, is second only to the National Gallery in its riches. It is, today, not really a single gallery but three different ones: a national gallery of British art, a gallery of modern sculpture, and a gallery of modern foreign paintings. The national collection pays special tribute to the work of Turner and Blake, the modern sculptures include

excellent examples of the work of Rodin, Eric Gill, Maillol, Mestrovic, Picasso, Epstein and Henry Moore, and its collection of the paintings of the Impressionist and post-Impressionist schools has an international reputation. Apart from these permanent treasures the Tate features special exhibitions which bring to London masterpieces from all over the world. The building—designed by Sidney R. J. Smith and opened in 1897—is in the imposing and artificial neoclassical style then prevailing. The public restaurant is decorated with remarkable *trompe l'oeil* murals by the late Rex Whistler. A much needed extension to the gallery is to be built on the adjacent site now occupied by a military hospital.

Television Centre for the British Broadcasting Corporation at Wood Lane, Shepherd's Bush, covers thirteen acres and is one of the largest television headquarters in Europe. The studios radiate from one side of a circular block and are designed to cope with everything foreseeable in this medium. Audiences are admitted to certain productions (see p. 35).

Temple is the name of the two Inns of Court—Inner and Middle Temples—which trace their origins to the mediaeval property of the Knights Templars. This military crusading order was suppressed in 1312 and the property later passed to the Knights Hospitallers of St. John of Jerusalem (p. 91). Meanwhile in the fourteenth century certain professors of the common law occupied the site and took in students to reside with them, thus beginning that legal community which has never left the Temple. Middle Temple

Hall dates from 1570 and has been excellently restored. Much of the original panelling, the carved Elizabethan screen, the magnificent double hammer-beams of the roof, the heraldic glass, and the serving table made from the timbers of Drake's *Golden Hind*, have been saved and replaced. It was in this hall that Shakespeare's own company acted *Twelfth Night* on February 2nd

1602. The Temple Church belongs to both Inns—it has an oblong chancel added to the original Norman 'round' church, one of the few remaining 'round' churches surviving in England. The recessed doorway is a perfect specimen of Norman carving. The many courts of the two Inns are peaceful refuges from the roar of London's traffic, and you reach them from Fleet Street by the dignified Wren gatehouse in Middle Temple Lane.

Temple Bar was removed in 1878 from its site at the west end of Fleet Street to the entrance of Theobalds Park at Cheshunt. It was built by Wren in 1670 to mark the City of London boundary. On it the heads of executed traitors were exposed. The site of Temple Bar was marked in 1880 by an obstructive and unworthy memorial carrying effigies of Queen Victoria and Edward VII (as Prince of Wales) and surmounted by a dragon, wrongly but familiarly known as 'The Griffin'. By ancient custom, which is still the practice, the sovereign visiting the City in state is met at Temple Bar by the Lord Mayor, who hands over the sword of state, which is immediately returned to him by the sovereign who then proceeds into the City.

Temple of Mithras was revealed during excavations in the City in 1954. It is a basilica, about 60 ft. long, dedicated to a Persian sun-god, who was adopted by the Romans in the first century. The Temple, one of the most important Roman relics in London, has been reconstructed near where it was discovered. The head of Mithras and other discoveries can be seen in the Guildhall Museum (p. 42).

Thames and the Riverside. London's river was once the main highway connecting the City of London and the royal fortress Tower with the royal palace of Westminster. It has rightly been described as 'liquid history'.

The Thames has always been popular with the do-it-yourself waterman and boats can be hired at almost every place of any size near the water. Craft of all kinds are to be had, from luxurious cruisers to skiffs and punts, not forgetting that odd hybrid, the motor punt.

River pleasure launches run from Westminster or Charing Cross Pier downstream to Greenwich or up to Hampton Court and hydrofoils link Tower Pier and Greenwich. Salters' Thames steamers run daily summer services from Kingston Bridge to Hampton Court and Windsor, and the Upper Thames can be explored by boat as far as Oxford. Let the Underground (and bus) be your boat train. If you explore the Thames upstream from Richmond in this way, you will be surprised how many of the small riverside towns have retained their unspoilt village character.

Almost all London's riverside attractions can be reached by using the towpath. You can walk along the path for over sixteen miles from Putney to Hampton Court; the path changes sides at Kingston. Between Kew and Richmond there is an entrance gate to Kew Gardens from the towpath running along the Surrey bank between Kew and Richmond.

The river Thames is home to many mute swans. They find the end of the towpath at Putney attractive, while others cruise around the Richmond and Teddington areas. London's swans belong to the Crown, and every year the colourful ceremony of Swan-Upping is carried out to check, count and register swans in the Thames reaches. It is done during the third week of July when the cygnets are about two months old.

Thames Tunnels. The first passenger tunnel under any river was cut under the Thames by the great Victorian engineer Sir Marc Isambard Brunel, and completed in 1843. It was intended as a road tunnel but is now used only by London Transport trains between Wapping and Rotherhithe. In 1897 the Blackwall Tunnel, cut by Sir Alexander Binnie, was opened for motor vehicles and pedestrians between Poplar and Greenwich. It is supplemented by a new twin tunnel. In 1902 a tunnel for pedestrians only was opened from Greenwich to Millwall. In 1908 the Rotherhithe Tunnel for vehicles and pedestrians between Stepney and Rotherhithe was opened. In 1912 a further tunnel was opened for pedestrians between North Woolwich and Woolwich. A tunnel between Purfleet and Dartford is open for vehicles (not pedestrians) on payment of a toll.

Tower Hill, although dominated by the Tower of London, has much to offer in its own right. A small chained-off square in Trinity Gardens marks the place at which 75 so-called traitors died. Fronting the Gardens is the memorial by Sir Edwin Lutyens to 12,000 men of the Merchant Navy and Fishing Fleets who were lost in the 1914–18 war and 'have no grave but the sea' and, behind it, its fellow by Sir Edward Maufe to the 26,000 lost in the last war. In Wakefield Gardens is one of the finest above-ground pieces of Roman wall in London. On the path called Tower Wharf between the Tower and the Thames are guns of all sizes, shapes and periods. From here the Honourable Artillery Company (p. 49) fires salutes. The path gives the best view of Tower Bridge. The companion ladder down to the water was once on the *Rawalpindi* which, in 1939 when an armed merchant cruiser, gallantly but hopelessly engaged two German warships and was sunk. Pepys tells of Tower Hill as a place of meetings. It is still 'speakers' corner' today. Many famous politicians and preachers hold lunch-hour meetings here which go on for as long as the audience can be kept from its work.

Tower of London, as built by William the Conqueror, was a simple central 'keep' (to overawe the Londoners and guard the Thames approaches) surrounded by walls and a moat. That keep is now the White Tower of a Tower of London that has received many additions during the succeeding centuries. Apart from its permanent role of fortress (it is still officially garrisoned by a Constable and Yeoman Warders) it was a royal palace until the days of James I, a prison until 1820, a mint until the nearby Royal Mint was built in 1810, a treasury (the Crown Jewels are still there), an observatory until

Greenwich was built in 1675, and for five centuries until 1834 it contained a royal menagerie. To know the history of the Tower is to study the darker side of England's story. Its prisoners have included a King of Scotland (1340–57), a King of France (1358–60), a King of England (Henry VI), queens, princes, pretenders, and a long list of nobles who have quarrelled with their sovereign and most of whom left the Tower only to walk to the headsman's block.

The Yeoman Warders still wear the picturesque uniform of Tudor days and will gladly take you round and tell you of the dramas behind these ancient stones. You will wish to see Traitors' Gate, which was the entrance to the Tower when the Thames was a highway between the royal palace at Westminster and the royal prison at the Tower. You will wish to see the Bloody Tower where it is believed the 'Little Princes' (Edward V and his brother the Duke of

York) were murdered, and where Sir Walter Raleigh spent thirteen years of reasonably comfortable imprisonment and occupied his time in writing his 'History of the World'. You will stand by the spot on Tower Green where two of Henry VIII's Queens were beheaded and where the pathetic tragedy of Lady Jane Grey was ended. You will shudder at the headsman's axe and block and the instruments of torture in the White Tower. And you will perhaps feel that Merrie England and the Good Old Days were not so merry and not so good . . .

To recover proportion the visitor should see before he goes the workmanship of the world's richest regalia, worthily displayed in a specially designed setting, and of our richest collection of armour; and the simple majesty of the Norman Chapel of St. John the Evangelist or the devoted renovation by modern architects and craftsmen of the Perpendicular Chapel of St. Peter ad Vincula. Certainly he should pay his respects to the Tower's ravens which hop tamely and happily where so much savage tragedy has been enacted.

Trafalgar Square was laid out to the design of Sir Charles Barry in 1829–41 to commemorate Nelson's victory and death on October 21st, 1805. It is dominated by the Nelson column designed by William Railton (1840–3) and surmounted by the statue of Nelson by E. H. Baily, nearly 18 feet high. The column of Devon granite has a total height of 184 feet 10 inches; the bronze lions at its base are the work of Sir Edwin Landseer (1868). Below the parapet on the National Gallery side are the Standard British Linear Measures let into the stonework. The fountains were completed in 1948 to the  original designs of Sir Edwin Lutyens. Water spouts from bronze groups by Sir Charles Wheeler and William McMillan. Trafalgar Square is a favourite terminal point for political demonstrations, its roosting starlings are a constant wonder to adults, and its pigeons are a never-failing attraction to children. A coin in a machine will obtain for you (and your immediate neighbours) a succinct talk about the Square and its neighbourhood.

Travel Enquiry Offices of London Transport are ready to answer all your travel problems. Please ask there for free maps and leaflets to help you enjoy your visit. Other London Transport publications are also on sale. There is a Travel Enquiry Office below the London Transport headquarters offices (p. 65) at St. James's Park Underground station. Others are at Piccadilly Circus, Oxford Circus, King's Cross, Victoria and Euston Underground stations. You may telephone Travel Enquiries at any time, day or night, by ringing 01-222 1234. London Transport posters and books are on sale at the Poster Shop, Griffith House, which is near Edgware Road Circle Line station.

Trial of the Pyx is the testing, on behalf of the monarch, of all coins turned out by the Royal Mint for public use. The tests have been the prerogative of the Goldsmiths' Company since the Middle Ages and they take place at Goldsmiths' Hall annually in March. Samples of coin, each denomination in its own box (called a 'pyx'), are sent to the Goldsmiths' Hall from the Royal Mint.

Trooping the Colour takes place annually on, or about, the monarch's official birthday (the first or second Saturday in June) on the Horse Guards Parade. It is the Londoner's favourite military display because it is so easy for all to see in reasonable comfort at one point or another between Buckingham Palace and the Horse Guards Parade, and perhaps because June is not usually without its sunshine. The Guards Division (p. 40) and the Household Cavalry (p. 51), in full dress, share the ceremony, during which the Queen's Colour is trooped before Her Majesty. The origin of the ceremony goes far back into military history and similar ceremonies take place wherever British troops are garrisoned.

Madame Tussaud's, near Baker Street station, is an exhibition of waxworks which originated with the work of a Dr. Curtius in Berne in 1757, and moved to Paris in 1762. In 1795, a descendant of the founder became Madame Tussaud. She was an excellent modeller in wax, and was commissioned to make death masks of many of the more famous victims of the French Revolution. She first opened an exhibition in London in 1802 which has been popular ever since, each year adding its quota of new models. Some of the models are originals, but the exhibition is worthy of a visit chiefly because of the accuracy of the costumes. Its Chamber of Horrors caters for that taste for the macabre common to most of us.

Tyburn, at Marble Arch, was for over 600 years the site of public executions. The first known was in 1169 and the last in 1783. From 1571 to 1759 a triangular gallows known as 'The Tyburn Tree' was a permanent structure near what is nowadays the southern end of the Edgeware Road. It is commemorated by Tyburn Way. In 1964 the actual site of the gallows was marked by a Portland stone slab placed on a traffic island at the junction of Bayswater Road and Edgware Road.

U

Unilever House, at Blackfriars, was designed by J. L. Simpson and Sir John Burnet, and opened in 1932. It is the headquarters of the world-wide Unilever organization whose products are used in every household. The equine groups of statuary at the east and west ends are by Sir William Reid Dick and the mermaid and merman over the east and west entrances by Gilbert Ledward.

University College, in Gower Street, was founded in 1826, and is the largest college in the University of London. Attached to the college is the Slade School of Fine Arts. The main buildings with a Corinthian portico and a fine dome (1827–8) are the work of William Wilkins, and they bear a striking resemblance to his National Gallery (p. 71). Beneath the dome is the **Flaxman Gallery** dedicated to John Flaxman (1755–1826), the first professor of sculpture at the Royal Academy. The college also displays the skeleton of Jeremy Bentham (1748–1832), whose philosophy inspired the founders of the College. The skeleton is dressed in Bentham's own clothes and seated in his chair.

University of London was founded in 1836 as an examining organization, and became a teaching university in 1900 with colleges and branches scattered over London and the Home Counties. It was the first British university to admit women to degrees (1878). Its headquarters are at the University site just north of the British Museum. The massive Senate House and Library dominate the site and were designed by Charles Holden. University College is just north of the site in Gower Street. King's College is in the Strand and occupies a wing of Somerset House. Other important colleges incorporated or affiliated include Bedford College in Regent's Park, the Imperial College of Science and Technology at South Kensington, the London School of Economics off Kingsway, Birkbeck College, and Goldsmith's College.

Variety for a change. London's summer visitors can enjoy old-fashioned Variety concert parties in local parks. They recapture the happy, breezy gaiety of the seaside 'pierrot show', an almost vanished world of variety without which no holiday was complete. At these fast-moving performances you can enjoy the patter and the dance (and learn what happened to the comedian on the way to the show) for a modest outlay. In some parks, you can take your partners for an evening of Old Time Dancing under the stars. Times and places from the Greater London Council Parks Department—01-836 5464—or local borough council offices.

Veteran Car Run. This run of early and curious automobiles commemorates the emancipation of the motorist from the 'man with a red flag in front of the vehicle' law which was rescinded in 1896. It takes place on the first Sunday in November, and usually starts from Hyde Park and finishes at Brighton.

Vickers Building is the superb tower block (1963) which dominates the London skyline at Millbank. Its 34 storeys of concrete and stainless steel rise to 387 feet, its shape is curiously curved, and its glass-clad façades reflect the changing sky. Its architects were Ronald Ward & Partners.

Victoria and Albert Museum, in Cromwell Road, South Kensington, has its origin in the Museum of Ornamental Art (1852) which was moved from Marlborough House and merged in the South Kensington Museum of 1857. It became the Victoria and Albert Museum in 1899. The present front was designed by Sir Aston Webb and the building was opened as the National Museum of Fine and Applied Arts. It contains priceless works of art magnificently displayed in two groups — 'primary' collections of 'masterpieces of all the arts brought together by style, period or nationality', and 'study' collections arranged according to material (ceramics, metalwork, textiles, woodwork, etc.). Among its special treasures are a fine collection of paintings and sketches by John Constable, the Raphael cartoons executed for Pope Leo x in 1516, and our best collection of English miniatures. Its print room is rich in etchings and engravings of the masters, and keeps very much in tune with contemporary movements in poster design and typography. The 'Victoria and Albert' has suffered from a title which suggests one rather undistinguished period in art—it is in fact a very large treasure house whose bewildering variety of exhibits from all periods is being brought into perspective and displayed to perfection by an enlightened and enterprising staff.

W

Wallace Collection is in Manchester Square, which lies behind Selfridge's in Oxford Street. The mansion was built in 1776–88 for the then Duke of Manchester and although it has been much altered since, is still an example of the great town house of the period. Its collection of great paint-  ings of many schools and periods, of miniatures (especially of the Napoleonic era), of furniture, of superb armour, of clocks, majolica and bric-à-brac, is both catholic and entertaining. By the terms of foundation, nothing can be added to (or more importantly, subtracted from) its treasures. The pictures include some excellent Dutch, four Rembrandts, examples of Rubens, Van Dyck, Holbein, Velasquez, Reynolds and Gainsborough, and much Watteau, Boucher, Fragonard and Greuze. The casual visitor will enjoy the Meissoniers and see the popular 'Laughing Cavalier' by Frans Hals, but he will certainly depart with a new admiration for, and understanding of, the tastes of the English eighteenth century at its cultured (and Francophile) best.

Waltham Abbey is officially the Abbey and Parish Church of Holy Cross and St. Lawrence at Waltham Holy Cross in Essex. There was a church on the site in Canute's day, but the nave of the present church is Norman on Saxon foundations and is only a part of the large mediaeval Augustinian Priory, the remains of whose gateway are just north of the church. Traditionally the body of King Harold was taken from the field of Hastings and buried here. It is a church overfilled with relics but nevertheless worthy of study. The nave has three tiers of arches supported by twelve huge Norman pillars, some cut with spiral and others with chevronned patterns as they are at Durham Cathedral. The small screen on the north of the nave and the Lady Chapel are fourteenth-century, and the large mural on the east wall is the work of an Augustinian monk of the early fifteenth century. The relics include a sixteenth-century parish whipping-post and pillory stocks, an Elizabethan fireplace, and some panelling from the neighbouring house (now demolished) where John Foxe wrote his *Book of Martyrs*. The exterior of the Abbey with its enormous old elm tree set in the heart of a typical Essex village, is most picturesque.

Waltham Cross is in the High Street of Waltham Cross, in Hertfordshire—it is one of the three remaining Eleanor Crosses. Originally twelve were erected by Edward I (1272-1307) to commemorate the places where the body of his Queen, Eleanor, rested on its journey from Harby in Nottinghamshire to her tomb in Westminster Abbey. The Waltham Cross has been restored but much of the original stone survives. The base supports three canopies each sheltering a new figure of the Queen. The original figures are preserved in Cheshunt Library.

Waterloo Place, at the bottom of lower Regent Street, has many memorials including the Guards Crimea Memorial by Bell (1859) (p. 26), the bronze statue of Florence Nightingale by Arthur Walker (1915) and the statue of Captain Scott carved by his widow (1915). Many of the plinths still show their bomb-scars from the last war. On the kerbsides are mounting blocks for horse riders placed there at the suggestion of the first Duke of Wellington.

Wellcome Institute of the History of Medicine, in Euston Road, was founded by Sir Henry Wellcome in 1913 and is a magnificent collection of over 200,000 exhibits dealing with the various aspects of the history of medicine and its related sciences. Five early pharmacies reconstructed with their contemporary equipment are a fascinating feature.

Well Hall, near Eltham Palace, for centuries belonged to the Roper family, into which Sir Thomas More's daughter Margaret married. The only surviving building is the brick Tudor Barn, whose upper floor is used as an art gallery for loan exhibitions. The roof timbers and the fireplace in the west wall are original. Well Hall Pleasaunce, as the gardens are called, has become one of South London's prettiest small parks.

Wellington Barracks, on the south side of St. James's Park, is a long post-Regency block of buildings built in 1833. In front is the parade ground, and near the main gate visitors can find the details for the Changing the Guard (p. 16) ceremonies.

Wellington Museum, at Apsley House, Hyde Park Corner, was for many years the town house of the first Duke of Wellington. The original mansion was built of red brick by Robert Adam for Baron Apsley, later

Lord Bathurst, between 1771 and 1778. The Duke of Wellington bought Apsley House after his victory at Waterloo. He carried out many alterations including the refacing of the house with stone, the addition of the Corinthian portico and the famous Waterloo Gallery. The house is now administered by the Victoria & Albert Museum. Its glittering treasures are for the most part illustrative of the doubtful taste of nineteenth-century Europe, but amongst the spoils, which the first Duke was allowed to retain after Napoleon's fall, are three superb Velasquez paintings which alone make a visit to Apsley House—sometimes known as 'No. 1 London'—more than worthwhile.

Wembley Stadium and Empire Pool. The Stadium was built as the colossal centre-piece of the British Empire Exhibition of 1924 and 1925. It accommodates 100,000 spectators under cover and was designed by J. W. Simpson and Maxwell Ayrton. It was used for the 1948 Olympic Games, and is the home of the F.A. Cup Final. The superb Empire Pool nearby, built by Sir Owen Williams and opened in 1934, was also used for the 1948 Olympics. 'Pool' is now a misnomer—it is a large sports hall catering for indoor sports such as tennis and table tennis, and spectacular ice-shows.

Wesley's Chapel and House, at 47 City Road, Finsbury, were built in the late eighteenth century. The Chapel (temporarily closed) has suffered from fire but has been faithfully restored. Wesley's simple tomb is in the centre of the churchyard at the rear of the Chapel. The house was built for Wesley and is now a Wesley Museum with many personal memorials of both John and Charles Wesley. Both Chapel and Museum are a centre of devoted pilgrimage for Methodists from all over the world.

Westminster Abbey. The official name is the Collegiate Church of St. Peter in Westminster, but to all Englishmen it is 'The Abbey'. It was founded by Edward the Confessor in 1065 as his burial place, and ever since it has been the mausoleum of our distinguished dead, both royal and commoner. The present building is mostly Early English Gothic of the time of Henry III (thirteenth century), but the Henry VII Chapel is, of course, pure

Tudor; the twin towers at the west end were designed by Wren's pupil Hawksmoor in 1740, and the north transept was completely remodelled to the designs of Sir George Gilbert Scott in 1884. Standing by the tomb of the Unknown Warrior, the glory of the loftiest nave in England can be appreciated to the full. Nearby, on the right, is the first contemporary portrait of an English king —Richard II, who was one of Westminster's most devoted patrons, and whose magnificent tomb

is in St. Edward's Chapel. If the visitor is wise he will not stop to study the clutter of memorials. He will find the simple slab in the north of side the nave which says 'O rare Ben Johnson' (mis-spelt), take a look at Chaucer's tomb in Poets' Corner in the south transept and pass on to the chancel. Here are the royal tombs with their magnificent effigies, the Coronation Chair dating back to 1307 when Edward I wished to accommodate Scotland's Stone of Scone, and the glories of Henry VII's Chapel with its banners of the Order of the Bath and its perfect fan vaulting. The cloisters and Chapter House should also be seen. All coronations since Norman times have taken place in the Abbey, but not all our kings have been buried there and none since George II in 1760. The Abbey was placed under an independent Dean and Chapter by Queen Elizabeth I and it remains so today.

Westminster Cathedral, near Victoria Station, is the seat of the Cardinal Archbishop of Westminster. It was designed by John Francis Bentley in the Byzantine style and the fabric was completed in 1903. Its tower is 284 feet to the top of the cross and commands a magnificent view of London—a lift takes visitors to

its gallery. The interior, which is of unpointed brick, will one day be completely lined with marbles and mosaics— a development which may spoil the impressive majesty of the widest nave in this country. Many of the side chapels have already been so completed. The Stations of the Cross are distinguished bas-reliefs by Eric Gill.

Westminster School, in Dean's Yard, is first on record in 1339 but was refounded by Queen Elizabeth I in 1560 In the Hall known as 'School' the annual ceremony of 'tossing the pancake 'takes place on Shrove Tuesday. The origin of the custom is unknown but it is thought to have started in the mid-eighteenth century. One boy from each form is chosen to compete. The pancake is tossed over the 'bar' and the boy retrieving the largest piece is rewarded with a guinea by the Dean. The tables in the dining-hall are said to have been made from timber of ships captured from the Spanish Armada.

Whitechapel Art Gallery was intended as a contribution to the cultural life of London's East End but the scope and enterprise of its exhibitions have given it wider fame. There is no permanent collection. The *art nouveau* front is by Townsend.

White City was first built in 1908 for the Olympic **Games** which were part of the Franco-British Exhibition. The original front entrance, next door to Shepherd's Bush (Central Line) Station, is an interesting survival of early exhibition technique, and the modern stadium in Wood Lane is our central stadium for athletics—it comfortably holds 50,000 spectators.

Whitehall takes its name from the old Whitehall Palace whose Banqueting House (p. 4) still commands this famous street of government buildings. The excellent equestrian statue at the Trafalgar Square end is of King Charles I—it was cast in 1633 and is the work of the Huguenot sculptor Le Sueur. The statue looks down Whitehall to the site of Charles's execution which took place on a specially erected platform at the north-west corner of the Banqueting House. On the right of Whitehall towards Parliament Square are the old Admiralty Building, the Horse Guards, the Treasury, and the Home Office. On the left are the Ministry of Agriculture, the Ministry of Defence, and the office of the Lord Privy Seal. Opposite the Home Office and dividing the busy traffic is the Cenotaph (p. 15) and just before is the most famous and least pretentious of all London streets—Downing Street (p. 28).

William Morris Gallery, at Lloyd Park, Walthamstow, is a gallery devoted to William Morris, the Victorian poet, artist-craftsman and socialist, who lived in Walthamstow from 1848 to 1856. It contains an interesting collection of Morris's original designs, a few personal relics, and specimens of craftsmanship from the Morris looms and printing presses. The gallery also includes the Brangwyn collection of pictures. That superb draughtsman Sir Frank Brangwyn was once a young craftsman employed by Morris, and he presented the gallery with many of his own works and also examples of the work of his contemporaries.

Wimbledon. To the world, Wimbledon means lawn tennis. Towards the end of June the world's greatest players meet at what is officially the 'All England Lawn Tennis and Croquet Club' in the annual championships, recognized as the most important open tournament in the game. The Centre Court accommodates 15,000 spectators.

Wimbledon Common is a thousand acres of natural heathland and silver-birch woodlands with three good lakes for winter skating and summer model-yachting. It was once the haunt of highwaymen preying on the Portsmouth Road, and there was a gibbet at the crossroads. Caesar's Camp in the south-west corner perpetuates a legendary connection with Cassivelaunus' campaign against Caesar, and the adjoining 'Roman' or 'Caesar's Well' has never been known to fail. The windmill in the centre of the Common was built in 1817 by a local carpenter, and, although it has long ceased to grind corn, its sails still turn merrily in the breeze. The common is large enough for a lengthy walk and there is a good scarlet-blazered golf club.

Woolwich was formerly celebrated for its **Royal Arsenal,** first established in 1716, now being swallowed up by G.L.C. development. On Woolwich Common is the **Royal Military Academy,** designed by Sir Jeffry Wyatville in 1805–8. Nearby is the **Rotunda Museum,** a circular building designed by Nash and originally erected in St. James's Park on the occasion of the visit of allied sovereigns to London in 1814. It now houses a good collection of early rockets, guns, muskets, rifles, arms of all kinds from all periods, together with some armour and ships' models. Crossing the river to North Woolwich is the **Woolwich Free Ferry,** first opened in 1889. It is served by three vessels of 740 tons capable of carrying 1,000 passengers and 200 tons of vehicles.

Yeomen of the Guard. The Queen's Bodyguard of the Yeomen of the Guard together with the Gentlemen-at-Arms (p. 37) are the sovereign's dismounted bodyguard and always a spectacular feature of state ceremonial. They have also certain traditional duties, the most

famous of which is the search of the vaults of the Houses
of Parliament before a state opening—a tradition which
dates from the discovery of the Gunpowder Plot in 1605.
The Bodyguard was first formed by Henry Tudor, Earl
of Richmond, on Bosworth Field in 1485 'for the protection of the dignity and grandeur of the English crown
forever'. The scarlet and gold Tudor uniforms are
exactly the same as those worn by the Yeomen Warders
at the Tower (p. 109), except that the Yeomen of the
Guard wear a cross belt in addition to the waist belt
worn by Yeomen Warders. It is their fine physique
that they owe their name of 'Beefeaters' (often wrongly
applied to Yeomen Warders)—a nickname first coined
by a visiting Grand Duke of Tuscany in 1669, although
a rival derivation is that the name is a corruption of
buffetiers du roy.

York House is now in use
as the municipal offices
of Richmond. It is a
simply designed red brick
house built in the late
seventeenth century, with
good panelling and a
beautiful staircase. Queen
Anne lived here as a child.
The riverside gardens display some remarkable
statuary.

Z

Zoo. The famous gardens of the Zoological Society of
London occupy the north side of Regent's Park. The
Society was first incorporated in 1829. The Zoo now
has a wild animal population of over 7,000, a magnifi-

cent aquarium, ample open space for the larger beasts, a fascinating Pet's Corner for the special entertainment of the children, and many architecturally exciting modern additions including Lord Snowden's aviary and Sir Hugh Casson's elephant house.

INDEX

1072/199RP/20M

HOW TO GET THERE

Addresses

Hours of opening

Prices of admission

Routes

LONDON TRANSPORT

55 Broadway, Westminster

SW1

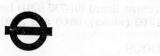

1973

A new edition appears each year

IMPORTANT NOTE

Every effort is made to ensure that the information given in this booklet is correct, but details are subject to alteration without notice.

BUS CHANGES

London's bus services are undergoing a major reorganization. As up-to-date details as possible are displayed on buses and at bus-stops. Not all the buses listed in this booklet run every day and some are more frequent than others. It is advisable to check your route by calling at a London Transport Travel Enquiry Office (see p. 30) or by telephoning Travel Enquiries (01-222 1234) at any time, day or night.

UNDERGROUND STATIONS

Certain Underground stations are closed at particular times of day, at weekends and on public holidays. See p. 52.

OPENING TIMES AND ADMISSION CHARGES

These are given as fully and accurately as possible according to information available when this booklet went to press. In the case of many national museums and galleries, admission charges are planned for 1973. Where known, these have been included. Value Added Tax will be introduced in April 1973, and will also affect many of the admission prices given in this book. For an up-to-date check telephone the London Tourist Board (01-730 0791) between 09 00 and 18 00 (winter), 08 00 and 20 00 (summer).

DOGS

Please note that in some places (Kew Gardens, for example) dogs are not allowed. If your dog is a keen sightseer, it may be worth enquiring beforehand.

† = National Trust Property.

Admiralty Arch The Mall, SW1
see *National Gallery*

Aer Lingus Terminal
see *Air Terminals*

Air Terminals
AER LINGUS
249 Brompton Road, SW3
Underground: South Kensington
Bus: 14, 30, 74, 74B
from 1 Feb London Tower
Hotel, Wrights Lane,
Kensington High St, W8
see *Commonwealth Institute*

BRITISH CALEDONIAN
Victoria Station, SW1
see *Victoria BR Station*

BEA
West London Air Terminal
Cromwell Road, SW7
Underground: Gloucester Road
Bus: 49, 74, 74B

BOAC
Buckingham Palace Road, SW1
Underground: Victoria
Bus: 11, 39

WEST LONDON
see *Air Terminals—BEA*

Albany Piccadilly, W1
Underground: Piccadilly Circus
Bus: 3, 6, 9, 9A, 12, 13, 14, 15,
19, 22, 38, 39, 53, 59, 88, 159,
505, 506

**Albert Hall and
Albert Memorial**
Kensington Gore, SW7
Underground: South Kensington
Bus: 9, 9A, 52, 73

Alexandra Palace and Park
Wood Green, N22
Underground: Finsbury Park
then bus W2, W3, W7; Wood
Green then bus W3

All Hallows-on-the Wall EC2
see *London's Wall*

All Hallows-by-the-Tower EC3
Underground: Tower Hill
Bus: 9A, 42, 78

All Saints' Church
Putney Bridge Approach,
Fulham, SW6
see *Fulham Palace*

All Soul's Church
Langham Place, Regent St, W1
see *Broadcasting House*

Apsley House
see *Wellington Museum*

Australia House Aldwych, WC2
ENQUIRIES, READING ROOM and
REFERENCE LIBRARY
Mons to Fris 09 00 to 17 15
Sats 09 00 to 12 00
Closed 26 Jan, Good Fri,
Sat & Mon at Easter, 25 Apr,
Spring & Late Summer Hol
Mons, Christmas Day,
Boxing Day. Free
Underground: Temple
Bus: 1, 1A, 4, 6, 9, 9A, 11, 13,
15, 55, 68, 77, 77A, 77B, 77C,
170, 171, 172, 176, 188, 196, 239,
502, 505, 513

Baden Powell House
Queen's Gate, SW7
Underground: South
Kensington, Gloucester Road
Bus: 49, 74, 74B

Bank of England
Threadneedle Street, EC2
Underground: Bank
Bus: 6, 8, 9, 11, 15, 21, 22, 25,
43, 76, 95, 133, 149, 501, 502

Banqueting House
Whitehall, SW1
Closed, re-opens Spring 1973
Tues to Sats 10 00 to 17 00
Suns 14 00 to 17 00. Closed Good
Fri. Open Easter weekend &

3

Mon, Spring & Late Summer
Hol Mons. Christmas plans
under review. 5p, children 2½p
see *Horse Guards*

Barbican EC2
Underground: Barbican
Bus: 4, 141, 279, 502

Battersea Park
Battersea, SW11
Underground: Sloane Square
then bus 137; South
Kensington then bus 39A, 45, 49
Bus: 19, 19A, 39, 44, 170, 249
see also *Festival Gardens*

BEA Air Terminal
see *Air Terminals*

Bedford College Inner Circle,
Regent's Park, NW1
Underground: Baker Street
Bus: 1, 2, 2B, 13, 18, 26, 27, 30,
59, 74, 74B, 113, 159, 176

Belfast, H.M.S. Symon's
Wharf, Vine Lane, off
Tooley St, SE1 2JH
Daily except Christmas Eve and
Day
11 00 to 18 00.   30p.
children 14 and under 20p,
pensioners 15p, pre-booked
parties: 20p, children 14 and
under 15p
British servicemen in
uniform free
Underground: London Bridge
Bus: 42, 47, 70, 78, 188

Berkeley Square W1
Underground: Green Park,
Bond Street
Bus: 25

Berwick Market
Berwick Street, Soho, W1
Mons to Sats
Underground: Piccadilly Circus
Bus: 14, 19, 22, 38

Bethnal Green Museum
Cambridge Heath Road, E2
Mons to Sats 10 00 to 18 00
Suns 14 30 to 18 00. Open
Easter weekend & Mon, Spring
& Late Summer Hol Mons
Closed Good Fri. Christmas Eve
& Day, Boxing Day. Admission
charges under consideration
Underground: Bethnal Green
Bus: 8, 8A, 106, 253

Billingsgate Market
Lower Thames Street, EC3
see *Monument*

Blackheath SE3
British Rail: Blackheath
Bus: 53, 54, 75, 89, 108, 108B,
192

Bloomsbury Squares WC1
BEDFORD SQUARE
Underground: Tottenham Court
Road
Bus: 1, 7, 8, 14, 19, 22, 24, 25,
29, 38, 73, 176

MECKLENBURGH SQUARE
Underground: Russell Square
Bus: 17, 18, 45, 46

BLOOMSBURY SQUARE
Underground: Holborn
Bus: 5, 7, 8, 19, 22, 25, 38, 55
68, 77, 77A, 77B, 77C, 170,
172, 188, 196, 239

RUSSELL AND TAVISTOCK SQUARES
Underground: Russell Square
Bus: 68, 77, 77A, 77B, 77C,
170, 188, 196, 239

BOAC Air Terminal
see *Air Terminals*

Boat Race Putney to Mortlake
Sat Apr 7
Underground: Putney Bridge,
Hammersmith, Ravenscourt
Park, Stamford Brook,
Turnham Green

4

British Rail: Putney, Barnes
Bridge, Mortlake
Bus: 9, 11, 14, 22, 27, 30, 33,
37, 72, 73, 74, 85, 85A, 91, 93,
220, 267, 290, E3

Bond Street
(Old and New Bond Streets), W1
Underground: Bond Street,
Green Park
Bus: 1, 6, 7, 8, 9, 9A, 12, 13, 14,
15, 19, 22, 25, 38, 59, 73, 88,
113, 137, 500, 505, 506, 616

Boston Manor House
Boston Manor Road,
Brentford
May to Sept, Sats only
14 30 to 17 00. 5p, children under
14 2½p. Grounds daily dawn to
dusk, free
Underground: Boston Manor
Bus: E1

British Caledonian Air Terminal
see *Air Terminals*

British Crafts Centres
43 Earlham Street,
Cambridge Circus, WC2H 9LD
Mons to Fris 10 00 to 17 00
(Thurs to 18 00), Sats 10 00 to
13 00. Closed Good Fri,
Easter Mon, Spring &
Late Summer Hol Mons,
Christmas Day, Boxing Day.
Free admission
Underground: Covent Garden
Bus: 1, 14, 19, 22, 24, 29, 38, 176

12 Waterloo Place,
Lower Regent St, SW1
Opening arrangements as above
see *Cinemas—Carlton*

**British Institute of
Recorded Sound**
29 Exhibition Road, SW7
Mons to Fris 10 00 to 13 30 and

14 30 to 18 00. Closed Good Fri,
Easter Mon, Spring & Late
Summer Hol Mons, Christmas
Eve and Day, Boxing Day. Free
Underground: South Kensington
Bus: 9, 14, 30, 45, 49, 52, 73,
74, 74B

British Museum
Great Russell Street,
WC1B 3DG
Mons to Sats 10 00 to 17 00
Suns 14 30 to 18 00. Closed
Good Fri, Christmas Eve
& Day. Open Easter weekend
& Mon, Spring & Late Summer
Hol Mons. Boxing Day plans
under review. Admission
charges under consideration
Underground: Tottenham
Court Road, Goodge Street,
Russell Square, Holborn
Bus: 68, 77, 77A, 77B, 77C,
170, 188, 196, 239 to Southamp-
ton Row (Great Russell Street);
7, 8, 19, 22, 25, 38, to New
Oxford Street (Museum Street);
172 to Southampton Place

MUSEUM OF MANKIND,
ETHNOGRAPHY DEPARTMENT
6 Burlington Gardens,
W1X 2EX
Times and charges as for
main museum.
Underground: Piccadilly Circus,
Green Park
Bus: see *Royal Academy*

**British Piano and
Musical Museum**
368 High Street, Brentford,
Middlesex (by tall gasholder)
Mar to Nov, Sats & Suns
(including Easter weekend)
14 30 to 17 00. 25p
Underground: South Ealing
then bus 65 or Gunnersbury
then bus 117, 267
Bus: E1, E2

British Theatre Museum
Leighton House,
12 Holland Park Road,
Kensington High Street,
W14 8LZ
Tues, Thurs and Sats 11 00
to 17 00. Closed Sat at
Easter, Christmas Day. Free
see *Leighton House*

Brixton Windmill
Blenheim Gardens, Brixton
Hill, SW2
Daily except Christmas Day
09 00 to dusk. 5p
Underground: Brixton, then
short walk up Brixton Hill
Bus: 50, 57A, 59, 95, 109, 133,
159

Broadcasting House (BBC)
Portland Place, W1
Underground: Oxford Circus
Bus: 1, 3, 6, 7, 8, 12, 13, 15, 25,
39, 53, 59, 73, 88, 113, 137,
159, 505, 616

Brompton Hospital
Fulham Road. SW3
Underground: South Kensington
Bus: 14, 39A, 45, 49

Brompton Oratory
Brompton Road, SW7
Underground: South Kensington
Bus: 14, 30, 74, 74B

Bruce Castle Museum
Lordship Lane, N17 8NU
Mons to Sats (closed Weds)
10 00 to 12 30 and 13 30 to
17 00. Closed Good Fri, Sat &
Mon at Easter, Spring & Late
Summer Hol Mons, Christmas
Day. Free
Underground: Seven Sisters
or Wood Green then bus 243

Buckingham Palace
The Mall, SW1
Underground: St James's Park,
Victoria, Hyde Park Corner,
Green Park
Bus: 2, 2B, 9, 9A, 10, 11,
14, 16, 19, 22, 24, 25, 26, 29,
30, 36, 36A, 36B, 38, 39, 52,
73 74, 74B, 137, 149, 181,
185, 500, 503, 506, 507
see also *The Queen's Gallery*

The Building Centre
26 Store Street, WC1E 7BT
Tel: 01-637 4522 (Information),
01-637 1022 (Administration)
Mons to Weds 09 30 to 17 30
Thurs 09 30 to 19 00
Fris 09 30 to 17 00.
Christmas Eve 09 30 to 12 00.
Closed Good Fri, Easter Mon,
Spring & Late Summer Hol
Mons, Christmas Day,
Boxing Day. Free
Underground: Goodge Street,
Tottenham Court Road
Bus: 14, 24, 29, 73, 176

Bunhill Fields Burial Ground
City Road, EC1
Underground: Old Street
Bus: 5, 43, 55, 76, 104, 141,
214, 243, 271

Burlington Arcade
Piccadilly, W1
Underground: Piccadilly Circus,
Green Park
Bus: 9, 14, 19, 22, 38, 506

Bush House Aldwych, WC2
see *Australia House*

Bushy Park
Teddington, Middlesex
Underground: Richmond
then bus 27, 270; Wimbledon
then bus 131, 155
Bus: 72, 111, 211, 216, 264, 267

Caledonian Market
Bermondsey Square,
Tower Bridge Road, SE1
Fridays

Underground: Elephant &
Castle then bus 1, 188
Bus: 42, 78

Camden Arts Centre
Arkwright Road,
Hampstead, NW3 6DG
Tues to Fris 11 00 to 20 00,
Sats (including Sat at Easter)
11 00 to 18 00, Suns 14 00 to
18 00. Closed Good Fri,
Easter Sun, Christmas Day,
Boxing Day
Underground: Finchley Road
Bus: 2, 2B, 13, 26, 113

Canada House
Trafalgar Square, SW1Y 5BJ

RECEPTION AND READING ROOM
Mons to Fris 09 30 to 17 00
Easter Mon, Spring and Late
Summer Hol Mon, 1 July,
3 Sep 09 30 to 12 00. Closed
Good Fri, Christmas Eve and
Day, Boxing Day. Free

REFERENCE LIBRARY
Mons to Fris 10 00 to 17 00
Closed Good Fri, Easter Mon,
Spring & Late Summer Hol
Mons, 1 July, 3 Sep, Christmas
Eve and Day, Boxing Day. Free
see *National Gallery*

**Canal-side Walk NW1 and
NW8,** Lisson Grove to
London Zoo
Dec to Feb (weather permitting)
Sats, Suns & public hols only
10 00 to 16 00. Mar to Nov Mons
to Sats 07 30 to sunset, Suns &
public hols 10 00 to sunset. No
cycles. No unaccompanied
children under 10
Bus: 59, 74, 74B, 159
see also *London Zoo*

Cannon Street BR Station EC4
Underground: Cannon Street
Bus: 9A, 18, 95, 149, 176A, 513

Canonbury Tower
Canonbury Place, N1
Underground: Highbury,
Essex Road
Bus: 4, 19, 30, 38, 43, 73, 104,
171, 271, 277, 279

Carlton House Terrace
The Mall, SW1
Underground: Trafalgar Square,
Piccadilly Circus
Bus: see *National Gallery*

†Carlyle's House
24 Cheyne Row, Chelsea, SW3
Closed until Aug.
Underground: Sloane Square
then bus 11, 19, 22; South
Kensington then bus 39A, 45, 49
Bus: 39

Carnaby Street W1
see *Theatres—Palladium*

Catford Stadium
Catford Bridge, SE6
Bus: 36, 36B, 47, 54, 75, 108B,
124, 141, 160, 180, 185

Caxton Hall Caxton Street,
Westminster, SW1
Underground: St James's Park
Bus: 10, 11, 24, 29, 39, 149,
503, 507

**Cecil Sharp House
(English Folk Dance and
Song Society)**
2 Regent's Park Road,
NW1 7AY
Mons to Sats 09 30 to 17 30
Closed Good Fri, Sat & Mon
at Easter, Spring & Late
Summer Hol Mons,
Christmas Day, Boxing Day
Free
Underground: Camden Town
then bus 74, 74B
Bus: 3, 53

Cenotaph Whitehall, SW1
see *Houses of Parliament*

Central Criminal Court
see *Old Bailey*

Central Hall Storey's Gate,
Westminster, SW1
see *Westminster Abbey*

Ceylon Tea Centre
22 Regent Street, SW1Y 4QD
Mons to Fris 10 00 to 18 30
Closed Good Fri, Easter Mon,
Spring & Late Summer Hol
Mons, Christmas Day, Boxing
Day
see *Albany*

Changing the Guard
THE QUEEN'S LIFE GUARD
Horse Guards, Whitehall, SW1
Mons to Sats at 11 00, Suns at
10 00. Inspected on foot at 16 00
see *Horse Guards*

THE QUEEN'S GUARD
Buckingham Palace, SW1
Daily at 11 30
see *Buckingham Palace*

Chapel Market Angel, N1
Daily (early closing on
Thurs and Suns)
Underground: Angel
Bus: 4, 19, 30, 38, 43, 73, 104,
171, 172, 214, 277, 279

Charing Cross Hospital
Agar Street, Strand, WC2
see *Charing Cross BR Station*

Charing Cross BR Station
Strand, WC2
Underground: Strand,
Trafalgar Square
Bus: 1, 1A, 6, 9, 9A, 11, 13, 15,
77, 77A, 77B, 77C, 170, 176, 505

Charlton House
Charlton Road, SE7

To view apply to the Warden,
01-856 3951. Grounds open
daily, free
British Rail: Charlton
Bus: 53, 54, 75

Charterhouse
Charterhouse Square, EC1
Underground: Barbican
Bus: 4, 5, 55, 243, 277, 279

Chelsea Old Church
All Saints, Cheyne Walk, SW3
Underground: South Kensington
then bus 39A, 45, 49
Bus: 11, 19, 22, 39

Chelsea Royal Hospital
Royal Hospital Road,
Chelsea, SW3 4SR
BUILDINGS and MUSEUM
Mons to Sats 10 00 to 12 00
& 14 00 to 16 30, Suns
14 00 to 16 30. Closed Good Fri,
Easter Sun, Christmas Day.
Open Sat & Mon at Easter,
Spring & Late Summer Hol
Mons, Christmas Eve,
Boxing Day. Free
Underground: Sloane Square
Bus: 11, 39, 137

Chenies Bucks
Underground: Chorleywood
then pleasant 1½ mile walk

Chessington Zoo and Circus
Chessington, Surrey
ZOO Daily except Christmas Day
09 30 (Nov to Feb 10 00) to
18 30 (Nov to Feb 16 00). Mar to
Sept 35p, children 14 & under
20p; Nov to Feb 15p, children
7½p. Pets Corner & Aquarium
extra, each 3p
CIRCUS 2 weeks at Easter &
from Whitsun to Sept
20p, children 10p
For other times tel. 39 27227

Underground: Richmond then
bus 65
British Rail: Chessington South
Bus: 71

Children's Hospital
Great Ormond Street, WC1
Underground: Russell Square
Bus: 17, 18, 45, 46, 68, 77, 77A,
77B, 77C, 170, 188, 196, 239

Chislehurst Caves Kent
Daily except Christmas Eve &
Day, Boxing Day 11 00 to 17 00
(Suns at 15 00 a Long Tour
17½p, children 10p)
12½p, children 14 & under 4p,
unaccompanied children 7½p
British Rail: Chislehurst
Bus: 61, 161, 161A, 227, 228

Chiswick House
Burlington Lane, Chiswick, W4
HOUSE Apr daily 09 30 to 13 00
& 14 00 to 17 30, May to Sept
daily 09 30 to 13 00 & 14 00 to
19 00, Mar & Oct Weds to Suns
only 09 30 to 13 00 & 14 00 to
17 30, Nov to Feb Weds to
Suns only 09 30 to 13 00 &
14 00 to 16 00. Open Good Fri,
Easter weekend & Mon, Spring
& Late Summer Hol Mons.
5p, children & pensioners 2½p
GROUNDS daily, free
Underground: Hammersmith
then bus 290
British Rail: Chiswick
Bus: E3

Chiswick Mall Chiswick, W4
Underground: Stamford Brook
Bus: 27, 91, 117, 267, 290, E3

Christie's Auction Rooms
8 King Street, SW1
Underground: Green Park
Bus: 9, 9A, 14, 19, 22, 25, 38, 506

Church House
Dean's Yard, SW1
see *Westminster Abbey*

Cinemas
ABC 1 & 2
Shaftesbury Avenue, W1
Underground: Tottenham Court
Road, Leicester Square
Bus: 1, 14, 19, 22, 24, 29, 38,
176

ACADEMY 1, 2 & 3
165 Oxford Street, W1
Underground: Oxford Circus
Bus: 1, 3, 6, 7, 8, 12, 13, 15, 25,
39, 53, 59, 73, 88, 113, 137,
159, 500, 505, 616

ASTORIA
157 Charing Cross Road, WC2
Underground: Tottenham Court
Road
Bus: 1, 7, 8, 14, 19, 22, 24, 25,
29, 38, 73, 176

BERKELEY
30 Tottenham Court Road, W1
see *Cinemas—Astoria*

BIOGRAPH
Wilton Road, SW1
see *Cinemas—Classic Victoria*

BLOOMSBURY
Brunswick Square, WC1
see Bloomsbury Squares—
Russell Square

CARLTON
Haymarket, SW1
Underground: Piccadilly Circus
Bus: 3, 6, 9, 9A, 12, 13, 14, 15,
19, 22, 38, 39, 53, 59, 88, 159,
505, 506

CASINO
Old Compton Street, W1
see *Cinemas—Columbia*

CENTA-CINEMA
Piccadilly, SW1
see *Cinemas—Carlton*

CINECENTA
Panton Street, SW1
see *Cinemas—Carlton*

CINEPHONE
Oxford Street, W1
Underground: Bond Street
Bus: 1, 2, 2B, 6, 7, 8, 12, 13,
15, 26, 30, 59, 73, 74, 74B, 88,
113, 137, 500, 505, 616

CLASSIC
91 Baker Street, W1
Underground: Baker Street
Bus: 1, 2, 2B, 13, 18, 26, 27,
30, 59, 74, 74B, 113, 159,
176

CLASSIC
Charing Cross Road, WC2
see *Cinemas—Odeon*
Leicester Square

CLASSIC
Piccadilly Circus, W1
see *Cinemas—Carlton*

CLASSIC MOULIN
Great Windmill Street, W1
see *Cinemas—Carlton*

CLASSIC POLY
Regent Street, W1
see *Cinemas—Academy*

CLASSIC VICTORIA
152 Victoria Street, SW1
Underground: Victoria
Bus: 2, 2B, 10, 11, 16, 24, 25,
26, 29, 36, 36A, 36B, 38, 39, 52,
149, 181, 185, 500, 503, 506, 507

CLASSIC WINDMILL
Great Windmill Street, W1
see *Cinemas—Carlton*

COLUMBIA
Shaftesbury Avenue, W1
Underground: Tottenham Court
Road, Leicester Square

CONTINENTALE
Tottenham Court Road, W1
see *Cinemas—Astoria*

CURZON Curzon Street, W1
see *Crewe House*

DOMINION
Tottenham Court Road, W1
see *Cinemas—Astoria*

EMPIRE AND EMPIRE TWO
Leicester Square, W1
see *Cinemas—Odeon,*
Leicester Square

EROS CARTOON CINEMA
Piccadilly Circus, W1
see *Cinemas—Carlton*

EVERYMAN Hampstead, NW3
Underground: Hampstead
Bus: 268

GALA ROYAL Edgware Road, W2
Underground: Marble Arch
Bus: 2, 2B, 6, 7, 8, 12, 15, 16,
26, 30, 36, 36A, 36B, 73, 74,
74B, 88, 137, 500, 505, 616

JACEY
Charing Cross Road, WC2
see *Cinemas—Astoria*

JACEY
Leicester Square, W1
see *Cinemas—Odeon*
Leicester Square

JACEY
Trafalgar Square, WC2
see *National Gallery*

LEICESTER SQUARE THEATRE
Leicester Square, W1
see *Cinemas—Odeon,*
Leicester Square

LONDON PAVILION
Piccadilly Circus, W1
see *Cinemas—Carlton*

METROPOLE
160 Victoria Street, SW1
see *Cinemas—Classic Victoria*

NATIONAL FILM THEATRE
NFT 1 and NFT 2
South Bank, SE1
Underground: Waterloo

Bus: 1, 1A, 4, 68, 70, 76, 149, 168A, 171, 176, 188, 196, 239, 501, 502, 503, 505, 507, 513

NEW VICTORIA
Vauxhall Bridge Road, SW1
see *Cinemas—Classic Victoria*

ODEON Haymarket, SW1
see *Cinemas—Carlton*

ODEON Leicester Square, WC2
Underground: Leicester Square
Bus: 1, 24, 29, 176

ODEON Marble Arch, W1
see *Cinemas—Gala Royal*

ODEON
St Martin's Lane, WC2
see *Cinemas—Odeon,
Leicester Square*

OSCAR I
Brewer Street, W1
Underground: Piccadilly Circus
Bus: 14, 19, 22, 38

PARAMOUNT AND UNIVERSAL
Regent Street, SW1
see *Cinemas—Carlton*

PARIS-PULLMAN
65 Drayton Gardens, SW10
Underground: Earl's Court,
Gloucester Road
Bus: 14, 30, 39A, 45

PRINCE CHARLES
Leicester Place, WC2
see *Cinemas—Odeon,
St Martin's Lane*

RIALTO Coventry Street, W1
see *Cinemas—Carlton*

STUDIO 1 & 2
225 Oxford Street, W1
see *Cinemas—Academy*

TIMES
Baker Street Station, NW1
see *Cinemas—Classic, Baker
Street*

VICTORIA CARTOON CINEMA
Inside Victoria Station, SW1
see *Cinemas—Classic Victoria*

WARNER RENDEZVOUS AND
WEST END
Leicester Square, WC2
see *Cinemas—Odeon,
Leicester Square*

City Information Centre
St Paul's Churchyard,
EC4M 8BX
Mons to Fris 09 30 to 17 00,
Sats 10 00 to 16 00 (10 00 to
12 30 Oct to Easter). Closed
Good Fri, Christmas Day,
Boxing Day. Free
Tel: 01-606 3030
Underground: St Paul's,
Mansion House
Bus: see *St Paul's*

City Temple
Holborn Viaduct, EC1
Underground: Chancery Lane
Bus: 8, 22, 25, 501

Clapton Stadium
Millfields Road, E5
Bus: 38, 48, 55, 256

Clarence House
Clarence Gate, The Mall, SW1
see *St James's Palace*

Cleopatra's Needle
Victoria Embankment, WC2
Underground: Charing Cross
Bus: 109, 155, 168, 168B, 172,
184

Club Row Market
Sclater Street, E1
Sunday mornings
Bus: 5, 6, 8, 22, 35, 47, 48, 67,
78, 149, 243A

College of Arms
Queen Victoria Street, EC4
Underground: Mansion House,
Blackfriars

11

Bus: 6, 9, 9A, 11, 15, 18, 76, 502, 513

Commonwealth Institute
Kensington High Street,
W8 6NQ
Mons to Sats 10 00 to 17 30
Suns 14 30 to 18 00
CINEMA Mons to Fris 12 15,
13 15, 15 00; Sats 14 45,
15 30, 16 25; Suns 15 00,
15 50, 16 40
Closed Good Fri, Christmas
Eve & Day, Boxing Day. Open
Easter weekend & Mon, Spring
& Late Summer Hol Mons
Free
Underground: High Street
Kensington
Bus: 9, 9A, 27, 28, 31, 33, 49, 73

Congress House
Great Russell Street, WC1
see *Bloomsbury Squares—
Bedford Square*

Conway Hall
Red Lion Square, WC1
see *Bloomsbury Squares—
Bloomsbury Square*

Corn Exchange
Seething Lane, EC3
Underground: Tower Hill
Bus: 10, 40, 40A

**County Hall (Greater London
Council)** SE1 7PB
For official business,
normal office hours Mons
to Fris. To view, Sats,
Easter Mon. Spring & Late
Summer Hol Mons 10 30 to
13 00 & 13 30 to 16 00
The public are admitted to
Council Meetings (alternate
Tues at 14 30, except during
holiday periods). Free

Underground: Westminster,
Waterloo
Bus: 12, 53, 59, 76, 77C, 109,
149, 155, 168A, 170, 171, 172,
184, 503, 507

Courtauld Institute Galleries
Courtauld-Warburg Building,
Woburn Square, WC1
Mons to Sats 10 00 to 17 00
Suns 14 00 to 17 00. Closed
Good Fri, Christmas Eve & Day
Boxing Day. Open Easter
weekend & Mon, Spring & Late
Summer Hol Mons. Free
Underground: Goodge Street,
Euston Square, Russell Square
Bus: 68, 77, 77A, 77B, 77C,
170, 188, 196, 239 to Woburn
Place; 14, 24, 29, 73, 176 to
Gower Street or Tottenham
Court Road

Covent Garden Market WC2
Underground: Covent Garden
Bus: 1, 6, 9, 9A, 11, 13, 15, 77,
77A, 77B, 77C, 176, 505

Crewe House
Curzon Street, Mayfair, W1
Underground: Green Park
Bus: 2, 2B, 9, 9A, 14, 16, 19,
22, 25, 26, 30, 36, 36A, 36B,
38, 73, 74, 74B, 137, 500, 506

Cricket
BLACKHEATH Kent
Rectory Field, SE3
Bus: 53, 54, 75, 89, 108, 108B,
192

BRENTWOOD Essex
Old County Ground
Bus: 247

ILFORD Essex. Valentines Park
Underground: Gants Hill
Bus: 62, 123, 129, 144, 145, 147,
148, 150, 167, 179

LEYTON Essex
Youth Sports Ground, E10
Underground: Leyton then
bus 34, 69, 278, or bus 58, 241
to Church Road then short
walk
Bus: 235

LORD's St John's Wood, NW8
Underground: St John's Wood
Bus: 2, 2B, 13, 26, 59, 74, 74B,
113, 159, 187

OVAL Kennington, SE11
Underground: Oval
Bus: 3, 36, 36A, 36B, 59, 95,
109, 133, 155, 159, 172, 185

ROMFORD Essex
Gallows Corner Sports Ground,
Gidea Park
Bus: 66, 87, 174, 246

Crosby Hall
Cheyne Walk, Chelsea,
SW3 5AZ
Throughout the year
Mons to Fris 10 00 to 12 00
& 14 15 to 17 00, Sats & Suns
14 15 to 17 00. Closed Good
Fri, Christmas Day, Boxing
Day. Free
Underground: South Kensington
then bus 45, 49
Bus: 11, 19, 22, 39, 39A

Crystal Palace Park and
National Sports Centre SE19
Underground: Brixton then bus
2B, 3
British Rail: Crystal Palace
Bus: 2B, 3, 12, 12A, 63, 108B,
122, 137, 154, 157, 227, 249

Cuming Museum Walworth
Road, SE17 1RS
Mons to Fris 10 00 to 17 30
(Thurs to 19 00). Sats

10 00 to 17 00. Closed Good Fri,
Easter Sat and Mon,
Spring & Late
Summer Hol Mons, Christmas
Day, Boxing Day. Free
Underground: Elephant &
Castle
Bus: 12, 17, 35, 40, 40A, 45, 68,
171, 176, 176A, 184, 196

Cutty Sark—see *Greenwich*

Dancing—Central London

CAFE DE PARIS BALLROOM
Coventry Street, W1
see *Cinemas—Carlton*

EMPIRE BALLROOM
Leicester Square, W1
see *Cinemas—Odeon,
Leicester Square*

HAMMERSMITH PALAIS
Shepherd's Bush Road, W6
Underground: Hammersmith
Bus: 9, 9A, 11, 27, 33, 72, 73,
74B, 91, 220, 266, 267, 290, 295

LYCEUM BALLROOM
Wellington Street, WC2
Underground: Strand, Temple
Bus: see *Theatres—Aldwych*

Dean's Yard
Westminster Abbey, SW1
see *Westminster Abbey*

The Design Centre
28 Haymarket, SW1 4SU
Mons to Sats including Sat at
Easter 09 30 to 17 30
(Weds & Thurs to 21 00).
Easter Mon, Spring & Late
Summer Hol Mons, Boxing
Day 14 30 to 18 30. Closed
Good Fri, Christmas Day. Free
Underground: Piccadilly Circus

Bus: 3, 6, 9, 9A, 12, 13, 14, 15, 19, 22, 38, 39, 53, 88, 159, 505, 506

Dickens House
48 Doughty Street, WC1N 2LF
Mons to Sats 10 00 to 17 00
Closed Good Fri, Sat & Mon
at Easter, Spring & Late
Summer Hol Mons, & a week at
Christmas. 15p, students 10p,
children 5p. Charges under
review
Underground: Russell Square
Bus: 19, 38. 55, 172 to Gray's
Inn Road or 17, 18, 45, 46 to
Guilford Street

Discovery, H.M.S.
Victoria Embankment, WC2
Daily except Christmas Day
13 00 to 16 30. Free
Underground: Temple
Bus: 109, 155, 168, 168B, 172,
184

Docks—see *Port of London*

Dogs Home Battersea
Battersea Park Road, SW8
Mons to Fris 09 30 to 17 00.
Sats, Suns, Good Fri, Easter
Mon, Spring & Late Summer
Hol Mons, Christmas Day,
Boxing Day 14 00 to 16 00 for
claims only. 10p, children 14
& under 5p
Underground: Vauxhall then
bus 44, 170

Donaldson Collection
see *Royal College of Music*

Down House
Downe. Kent, BR6 7JT
Daily except Mons, Fris &
Christmas Day 11 00 to 17 00.
30p, children 15 & under 10p
Bus: 146 (from Bromley)

Downing Street Whitehall, SW1
see *Horse Guards*

Duke of York's Column
The Mall, SW1
Underground: Trafalgar Square,
Piccadilly Circus
Bus: see *National Gallery*

**Dulwich College Picture
Gallery** College Road, SE21
Tues to Sats: May to Aug
10 00 to 18 00; Sept 1 to Oct 15
& Mar 16 to Apr 30, 10 00 to
17 00; Oct 16 to Mar 15, 10 00
to 16 00. Suns: May to Aug
14 00 to 18 00; Apr & Sept
14 00 to 17 00. Open Sat & Sun
at Easter. Closed Good Fri & a
few days at Christmas
10p (July & Aug 20p), children
15 & under 5p. Season ticket
£1, children 50p
Underground: Brixton then
bus 3 to Thurlow Park Road
British Rail: West Dulwich
Bus: 37, P4 to Dulwich
Village; 12, 12A, 78, 176,
176A, 185 to Dulwich Library

Earl's Court Exhibition Hall
Warwick Road, SW5
Underground: Earl's Court,
West Brompton
Bus: 30, 31, 74, 74B

Elfin Oak
Kensington Gardens, W8
Underground: Queensway,
Bayswater
Bus: 12, 88

Eltham Palace
Court Yard, Eltham, SE9
Thurs and Suns. May to Oct
11 00 to 19 00, Nov to Apr
11 00 to 16 00. Open Easter Sun,
closed Christmas Eve & Day,
Boxing Day. Free

British Rail: Eltham
(Well Hall)
Bus: 21, 21A, 61, 89, 108, 124,
124A, 126, 132, 160, 160A, 161,
161A, 227, 228, B1

Ely House
Dover Street, W1
Mons to Fris 09 30 to 17 30
Closed Good Fri, Easter Mon,
Spring & Late Summer Hol
Mons, Christmas Day,
Boxing Day. Free
Underground: Green Park
Bus: 9, 9A, 14, 19, 22, 25, 38, 506

Ely Place
Charterhouse Street, EC1
Underground: Chancery Lane,
Farringdon
Bus: 8, 17, 18, 22, 25, 45, 46, 63,
168A, 221, 243, 259, 501

Epping Forest Essex
Underground: Loughton,
Theydon Bois, Epping or
Walthamstow Central then
British Rail to Chingford
Bus: 20, 20A, 69, 102, 121, 145,
167, 167A, 179, 191, 205A,
217A, 235, 242, 250, 254, 262

**Epsom and Epsom Downs
Racecourse** Epsom, Surrey
Underground: Morden then bus
164, 293 to Epsom or 164A to
Tattenham Corner
British Rail: Epsom, Epsom
Downs, Tattenham Corner

Euston BR Station NW1
Underground: Euston,
Euston Square
Bus: 14, 18, 30, 68, 73, 77,
77A, 77B, 77C, 170, 188,
196, 239

Fairfield Halls
Park Lane, Croydon, Surrey
Bus: 12A, 50, 54, 64, 68, 109,
119, 119A, 119B, 130, 130A,
130B, 166, 166A, 194, 194B,
197, 197A, 197B, 233, C1, C2,
C3, C4

Fat Boy Cock Lane, EC4
Underground: St Paul's
Bus: 8, 22, 25, 277, 279, 501

Fenchurch Street BR Station
EC3
Underground: Tower Hill
Bus: 9A, 10, 15, 25, 40, 40A,
42, 44, 78, 95

†Fenton House
Hampstead Grove,
Hampstead, NW3
Closed until June 1973
Underground: Hampstead
Bus: 210, 268

Festival Gardens and Fun Fair
Battersea Park, SW11
Daily Apr to Sept afternoons
& evenings (& from 10 30
Easter Mon & Spring & Late
Summer Hol Mons). Gardens
free. Admission to Fun Fair 3p
see *Battersea Park*

Fleet Street EC4
Underground: Blackfriars
Bus: 4, 6, 9, 9A, 11, 15, 171,
502, 513

**Football—Association
(Professional)**

ARSENAL
Arsenal Stadium,
Highbury, N5
Underground: Arsenal
British Rail: Finsbury Park
Bus: 4, 19, 236

15

BRENTFORD
Griffin Park, Brentford,
Middlesex
Underground: South Ealing
then bus 65 or short walk
British Rail: Brentford Central
Bus: 91, 116, 117, 267, E1, E2

CHARLTON ATHLETIC
The Valley, SE7
British Rail: Charlton
Bus: 177, 180, 180A

CHELSEA
Stamford Bridge, SW6
Underground: Fulham
Broadway
Bus: 11, 14, 22, 28, 91, 295

CRYSTAL PALACE
Selhurst Park, SE25
British Rail: Selhurst
Norwood Junction, Thornton
Heath
Bus: 50, 68, 75, 119A, 130A,
130B, 154, 157, 159, 190, 194B

FULHAM
Craven Cottage, SW6
Underground: Putney Bridge
Bus: 30, 74, 220

MILLWALL
The Den, New Cross, SE14
Underground: New Cross Gate
Bus: 21, 36, 36A, 36B, 53, 141,
171, 177, 180A, P1

ORIENT
Leyton Stadium,
Brisbane Road, E10
Underground: Leyton
Bus: 34, 58, 69, 236, 241, 278

QUEEN'S PARK RANGERS
Loftus Road, W12
Underground: Shepherd's Bush
(Metropolitan Line),
White City
Bus: 12, 49, 105, 207, 220

TOTTENHAM HOTSPUR
White Hart Lane, N17
Underground: Seven Sisters

then bus 97, 149, 259, 279
or Wood Green then bus W3
British Rail: White Hart Lane

WATFORD
Vicarage Road, Watford, Herts
Underground or British Rail:
Watford High Street
Bus: 142, 258

WEST HAM UNITED
Boleyn Ground,
Upton Park, E13
Underground: Upton Park
Bus: 5, 15, 23, 40, 58, 162, 238,
S1

**Football—Association
(Amateur and Non-League
Professional)**
BARKING Vicarage Field,
Ripple Road, Barking
Underground: Barking
Bus: 23, 62. 87. 162, 169, 179,
193, 199, 238, 291

BARNET Underhill,
Barnet, Herts
Underground: High Barnet
Bus: 34, 84, 107, 134, 263

BROMLEY
Hayes Lane, Bromley. Kent
British Rail: Bromley South
Bus: 119, 119A, 146

CLAPTON Spotted Dog Ground,
Upton Lane, E7
Underground: Plaistow then
bus 278
British Rail: Forest Gate

CORINTHIAN-CASUALS
see *Football, Association—
Tooting and Mitcham United*

DULWICH HAMLET
Champion Hill,
Dog Kennel Hill, SE22
Underground: Elephant & Castle
then bus 176, 184, or Oval
then bus 185

British Rail: East Dulwich,
Denmark Hill

ENFIELD The Stadium,
Southbury Road,
Enfield, Middlesex
Underground: Turnpike Lane
then bus 217, 231
British Rail: Enfield Town,
Southbury Road
Bus: 107, 121, 135, 135A,
191, 217A

HAYES Church Road,
Hayes, Middlesex
British Rail: Hayes and
Harlington
Bus: 90B, 98, 195, 204, 273

HENDON Claremont Road,
Cricklewood. NW2
Underground: Brent
Bus: 112, 113, 212, then a
half-mile walk

HILLINGDON BOROUGH
Leas Stadium, Falling Lane,
Yiewsley
Underground: Uxbridge then
bus 222, 224, 224B
British Rail: West Drayton
and Yiewsley
Bus: 223

ILFORD Lynn Road, Newbury
Park, Essex
Underground: Newbury Park
Bus: 66, 139, 169, 169A

KINGSTONIAN Thorpe Road,
Richmond Road,
Kingston-upon-Thames, Surrey
Underground: Richmond then
bus 65, 71
British Rail: Kingston

LEYTONSTONE Granleigh Road,
Leytonstone, E11
Underground: Leytonstone
Bus: 10, 236, 262

ROMFORD Brooklands Road,
Romford, Essex
Underground: Dagenham
Heathway then bus 174, 175
British Rail: Romford
Bus: 66, 66B, 86, 87, 103, 165
193, 247, 247A, 248, 250, 252,
294

SOUTHALL Western Road,
Southall, Middlesex
British Rail: Southall
then bus 105, 195
Bus: 120, 232, then a short walk

SUTTON UNITED
Borough Sports Ground,
Gander Green Lane,
Sutton, Surrey
British Rail: West Sutton
Bus: 80, 80A direct, or
154, 164, 164A, 280 to
Sutton Green then a short walk

TOOTING AND MITCHAM UNITED
CORINTHIAN-CASUALS
Sandy Lane, Mitcham, Surrey
Underground: Tooting
Broadway then bus 44, 64, 77,
88, 280
British Rail: Tooting
Bus: 115

WALTHAMSTOW AVENUE
Greenpond Road,
Walthamstow, E17
Underground: Blackhorse Road
Bus: 58, 123, 256

WEALDSTONE Lower Mead,
Station Road,
Wealdstone, Middlesex
Underground: Harrow-on-the-
Hill
British Rail: Harrow &
Wealdstone, then bus 114, 182,
186, 258, 286

WIMBLEDON
Plough Lane, SW19
Underground: Wimbledon,
Wimbledon Park

British Rail: Haydons Road
Bus. 77A, 77C, 200

Football—Rugby
BLACKHEATH Rectory Field,
Blackheath, SE3
Bus: 53, 54, 75, 89, 108, 108B,
192

ESHER Rugby Ground,
Molesey Road,
Hersham, Surrey
Bus: 264

HARLEQUINS
Twickenham and Stoop
Memorial Ground,
Craneford Way, Twickenham
see *Football, Rugby—RFU
Ground*

LONDON IRISH The Avenue,
Sunbury-on-Thames
British Rail: Sunbury
Bus: 90, 216, 237, 264

LONDON SCOTTISH
RICHMOND
Richmond Athletic Ground,
Twickenham Road, Richmond
Underground or British Rail:
Richmond
Bus: 27, 65, 71, 90, 90B, 202,
270, 290

LONDON WELSH Old Deer Park,
Kew Road, Richmond
Underground or British Rail:
Richmond
Bus: 27, 65, 71, 90, 90B, 202,
270, 290

METROPOLITAN POLICE
Imber Court, East Molesey
British Rail: Esher
Bus: 72, 131, 155, 201, 206, 211

RICHMOND
see *Football, Rugby—London
Scottish*

ROSSLYN PARK Priory Lane,
Upper Richmond Road,
Roehampton
Underground: Hammersmith
then bus 33, 72, 73
Bus: 37

RFU GROUND
Whitton Road, Twickenham
Underground: Richmond then
bus 33
Bus: 267, 281

ST MARY'S HOSPITAL
Udney Park Road, Teddington
Bus: 27, 270, 281, 285

SARACENS Green Road,
Southgate, N14
Underground: Southgate then
bus 298, 299
Bus: 107

STREATHAM AND CROYDON
Brigstock Road,
Thornton Heath
Bus: 50, 59, 109, 115, 119A,
130, 130A, 130B, 166, 190,
194B, 197A, 289

WASPS Repton Avenue,
Eton Avenue, Sudbury
Underground: Sudbury Town
Bus: 18, 92, 182, 245, 245A

WOODFORD Highams, High
Road, Woodford Green
Underground: Snaresbrook
then bus 20A
Bus: 20, 179, 275

Forty Hall
Forty Hill, Enfield
Tues to Fris & Easter Mon &
Spring & Late Summer Hol
Mons 10 00 to 20 00, Sats &
Suns (including Easter
weekend) 10 00 to 18 00
Closes 17 00 Oct to Easter.
Closed Good Fri, Christmas
Day, Boxing Day. Free

Underground: Turnpike Lane
then bus 231
Bus: 135, 135A

**Foundling Hospital Art Gallery
and Museum**
40 Brunswick Square,
WC1N 1AZ
Mons and Fris only, 10 00 to
12 00 & 14 00 to 16 00. Closed
Good Fri, Easter Mon, Spring
& Late Summer Hol Mons,
Christmas Day. 10p
see *Bloomsbury Squares—
Russell Square*

Freemason's Hall
Great Queen Street, WC2
Underground: Holborn,
Covent Garden
Bus: 7, 8, 19, 22, 25, 38, 55, 68,
77, 77A, 77B, 77C, 170, 172,
188, 196, 239, 501

Friends House
Euston Road, NW1 2BJ
To view, write to the
Secretary, Society of Friends
Underground: Euston,
Euston Square
Bus: 14, 18, 30, 68, 73, 77,
77A, 77B, 77C, 170, 188, 196,
239

Fulham Palace and Bishop's
Park Fulham, SW6
Underground: Putney Bridge
Bus: 14, 22, 30, 74, 85, 85A, 93,
220

Gardening Centre Syon Park,
Brentford, Middlesex
Daily except Christmas Day &
Boxing Day. 25 Mar to 30 Oct
10 00 to 18 00 (last admission
17 00), 31 Oct through winter
10 00 to 16 00 or dusk if earlier
(last admission 15 00).
20p, pensioners & children 16

& under 15p (From 1 April
1973 30p, pensioners and
children 16 & under 20p),
children 2 & under free
Aviary and Aquarium 12p
see *Syon House*

Geffrye Museum
Kingsland Road,
Shoreditch, E2 8EA
Tel: 01-739 8368
Tues to Sats (including Sat
at Easter) & Easter Mon,
Spring & Late Summer Hol
Mons 10 00 to 17 00. Suns
(including Easter Sun) 14 00
to 17 00. Closed Good Fri,
Christmas Day, Boxing Day
Free
Underground: Liverpool Street
then bus 22, 48, 97, 149
Bus: 67, 243, 243A

Geological Museum
Exhibition Road, SW7
Mons to Sats 10 00 to 18 00
Suns 14 30 to 18 00. Closed
Good Fri, Christmas Eve &
Day, Boxing Day. Open Sat,
Sun & Mon at Easter, Spring
& Late Summer Hol Mons.
10p (July & Aug 20p)
pensioners & children 14 &
under 5p
see *Science Museum*

†George Inn
Borough High Street, SE1
Underground: London Bridge
Bus: 8A, 10, 18, 21, 35, 40,
40A, 43, 44, 47, 48, 70, 133,
501, 513

Gipsy Moth IV—see *Greenwich*

Golders Hill Park
Golders Green, NW11
Underground: Golders Green
then bus 210, 268

19

Goldsmiths' Hall
Foster Lane, Cheapside, EC2
Underground: St Paul's
Bus: 4, 8, 22, 25, 141, 501, 502

Grange Farm Camp
Chigwell Road, Chigwell, Essex
Underground: Chigwell, then bus 167A

Gray's Inn WC1
HALL, CHAPEL and LIBRARY
to view, write to the
Under Treasurer
GARDENS May, June, July,
Mons to Fris 12 00 to 14 00;
Aug & Sept, Mons to Fris
09 30 to 17 00
Closed Good Fri, Easter Mon,
Spring & Late Summer Hol
Mons, Christmas Day, Boxing
Day. Free (children not
admitted)
Underground: Chancery Lane
Bus: 8, 17, 18, 19, 22, 25, 38,
45, 46, 55, 171, 172, 501

Green Park SW1
Underground: Green Park
Bus: 2, 2B, 9, 9A, 14, 16, 19,
22, 25, 26, 30, 36, 36A, 36B, 38,
52, 73, 74, 74B, 137, 500, 506

Greensted Church
near Ongar, Essex
Underground: Blake Hall
or Ongar then pleasant
1¼ mile walk

Greenwich SE10

CUTTY SARK Greenwich Pier
Mons to Sats including Sat at
Easter 10 00 to 17 00, Suns
including Easter Sun 14 30 to
17 00 (to 18 00 in summer).
Easter Mon 11 00 to 17 00,
Spring & Late Summer Hol

Mons 11 00 to 18 00. Good Fri,
Boxing Day 14 30 to 17 00
Closed Christmas Eve & Day
15p, children 14 & under 8p
(unaccompanied children not
admitted)

GIPSY MOTH IV Greenwich Pier
Hours as Cutty Sark
10p, children 14 & under
(must be accompanied) 5p

GREENWICH CHURCH High Road

NATIONAL MARITIME MUSEUM
including QUEEN'S HOUSE
Mons to Sats including Sat &
Mon at Easter, Spring & Late
Summer Hol Mons 10 00 to
18 00 (17 00 in Winter),
Suns including Easter
Sun 14 30 to 18 00. Closed
Good Fri, Christmas Eve &
Day, Boxing Day. Entry fee
(admitting also to Old Royal
Observatory) 10p (July & Aug
20p), children 15 & under 5p;
season ticket £1, children 50p

OLD ROYAL OBSERVATORY
(Flamsteed House)
Greenwich Park
Times as for rest of National
Maritime Museum with Winter
closing at 17 30
Museum entry fee admits
also to Observatory

PLANETARIUM
Public programme during
school hols on Mons, Tues,
Thurs, Fris (not Good Fri,
Christmas Day or Boxing Day)
also on 1st & 3rd Sats of
month in summer, 14 30
15p, children 5p

ROYAL NAVAL COLLEGE
Park Row
PAINTED HALL and CHAPEL
daily except Thurs 14 30 to 17 00
Closed Good Fri, Christmas

Eve & Day, Boxing Day. Open
Sat, Sun & Mon at Easter,
Spring & Late Summer Hol
Mons. Free
Underground: Surrey Docks
then bus 1A, 70, 108B, 188
British Rail: Maze Hill
Bus: 53, 54, 75, 177, 180, 180A,
185

Grosvenor Square W1
Underground: Bond Street,
Marble Arch
Bus: 1, 6, 7, 8, 12, 13, 15, 59,
73, 88, 113, 137, 505, 616 to
Selfridge's; 2, 2B, 16, 26, 30,
36, 36A, 36B, 73, 74, 74B,
137 to Grosvenor Gate; 25 to
Brook Street; 500

Guards Museum
Wellington Barracks,
Birdcage Walk, SW1
Mons to Sats (including
Sat at Easter) 10 00 to 17 00,
Suns (including Easter Sun)
& Easter Mon & Spring &
Late Summer Hol Mons
11 30 to 13 30 & 14 30 to 17 00.
Nov to Feb closes daily 16 00
Closed Good Fri, Christmas
Eve & Day, Boxing Day. 5p
Unaccompanied children
not admitted
Underground: St James's Park
Bus: 10, 11, 24, 29, 39, 149,
503, 507

Guildhall
Corporation of London,
King Street, EC2

REFERENCE LIBRARY Mons to
Sats 09 30 to 17 00. Closed
Good Fri, Sat & Mon at Easter,
Spring & Late Summer Hol
Mons, Christmas Day,
Boxing Day. Free

ART GALLERY (closed between
exhibitions) Mons to Sats

10 00 to 17 00. Closed
Good Fri, Sat & Mon at Easter,
Spring & Late Summer Hol
Mons, Christmas Day,
Boxing Day. Usually free

GREAT HALL Mons to Sats
including Sat at Easter
10 00 to 17 00
Spring & Late Summer Hol
Mons 14 00 to 17 00), Easter
Sun & Suns May to Sept
14 00 to 17 00. Closed
Good Fri, Easter Mon,
Christmas Day, Boxing Day
Free

MUSEUM Gillett House,
Bassishaw High Walk,
Basinghall Street, off
London Wall
Mons to Sats 10 00 to 17 00
Closed Good Fri, Sat & Mon at
Easter, Spring & Late Summer
Hol Mons, Christmas Day,
Boxing Day. Free

EXHIBITION HALL Basinghall
Street, behind Guildhall
(closed between exhibitions)
Mons to Fris 10 00 to 17 00
(Weds to 19 00). Closed
Good Fri, Easter Mon, Spring
& Late Summer Hol Mons,
Christmas Day, Boxing Day
Free
Underground: Bank, Mansion
House, Moorgate (for Museum
and Exhibition Hall)
Bus: 6, 8, 9, 9A, 11, 15, 21, 22,
25, 43, 76, 95, 133, 501, 502,
513
see also *City Information Centre*

**Gunnersbury Park and
Museum, W3**
PARK daily, free
MUSEUM Apr to Sept Mons to
Fris (including Easter Mon,
Spring & Late Summer Hol
Mons) 14 00 to 17 00, Sats &

Suns (including Easter
weekend) 1400 to 1800.
Oct to Mar daily 1400 to 1600
Closed Good Fri, Christmas
Day, Boxing Day. Christmas
Eve plans variable. Free
Underground: Acton Town
Bus: 15, 91, E3

Guy's Hospital
St Thomas's Street, SE1
Underground: London Bridge
Bus: 8A, 10, 18, 21, 35, 40,
40A, 43, 44, 47, 48, 70, 133,
501, 513

Hackney Stadium
Waterden Road, Stratford, E15
Bus: 6, 30, S3 to
Hackney Wick; 236

Hadley Church
near Barnet
Underground: High Barnet
then bus 134

Hainault Forest
Underground: Hainault then
bus 62, 150, 247A
Bus: 62, 150, 247A

Ham Common
near Richmond, Surrey
Underground: Richmond then
bus 65, 71

†Ham House
near Richmond, Surrey
HOUSE Apr to Sept Tues to Suns
(including Sat & Sun at Easter)
& Easter Mon & Spring & Late
Summer Hol Mons 1400 to
1800. Oct to Mar Tues to
Suns 1200 to 1600. Closed
Good Fri, Christmas Day,
Boxing Day. 20p, pensioners &
children 16 & under 10p
(unaccompanied children
under 12 not admitted)

GROUNDS daily, free
see *Ham Common*

Hammersmith Mall
Upper and Lower Mall, W6
Underground: Ravenscourt
Park
Bus: 9, 9A, 27, 33, 72, 73, 91,
255, 267, 290

Hampstead Garden Suburb
Underground: Golders Green or
East Finchley then bus 102, 244

Hampstead Heath NW3
Underground: Hampstead,
Golders Green
Bus: 24, 46, 187, 210, 268, C11

Hampton Court Palace
Middlesex

PARK AND GARDENS
King's Privy Garden, Great
Fountain Gardens .Tudor and
Elizabethan Knot Gardens,
Broad Walk and Wilderness
daily until 2100, or dusk if
earlier. Free

STATE APARTMENTS & GREAT
HALL (admissions cease 30 mins
before closing time)
Mons to Sats: May to Sept
0930 to 1800, Oct 0930 to 1700,
Nov to Feb 0930 to 1600,
Mar & Apr 0930 to 1700.
Suns: May to Sept 1100 to
1800, Mar & Apr & Oct 1400
to 1700, Nov to Feb 1400 to
1600. Closed Good Fri,
Christmas Eve & Day,
Boxing Day. Open Easter
weekend & Mon, Spring &
Late Summer Hol Mons

BANQUETING HOUSE, GREAT
KITCHEN & CELLARS & TUDOR
TENNIS COURT
Apr to Sept only. Times as above
VINE Times as for State
Apartments

MAZE daily 09 30 to 15 mins
before closing of gardens
Admission to all parts of
palace open to public,
including Vine & Maze, 20p
(from 1 April 1973 30p) (Oct to
Mar 10p), pensioners &
children under 16 5p (from
1 April 1973 10p). Vine
only, 1p. Maze only, 2p
Bus: 72, 111, 131, 155, 201, 206,
211, 216, 264, 267

Harefield Church Middlesex
Underground: Northwood or
Uxbridge then London
Country bus

Harringay Stadium
Green Lanes, N4
Underground: Manor House
Bus: 29, 141, 171, 221, 298

Harrow School and Church
Harrow-on-the-Hill, Middlesex
OLD SCHOOLS, SPEECH ROOM,
CHAPEL, AND WAR MEMORIAL
BUILDING
To view, telephone the Custos
(01-422 1455)
Underground: Harrow-on-the-
Hill
Bus: 114, 136, 140, 182, 183

Hayward Gallery (Arts Council)
South Bank, SE1
Mons to Sats 10 00 to 18 00
(Tues and Thurs till 20 00)
Suns 12 00 to 18 00
Closed Christmas Eve & Day,
Boxing Day. Open Good Fri,
Easter weekend & Mon, Spring
& Late Summer Hol Mons
Closed between exhibitions
Admission charges vary
see *Royal Festival Hall*

Heathrow Airport Middlesex
ROOF GARDENS daily except
Christmas Day & Boxing Day

10 00 to dusk. 15p, children
15 & under 5p. Charges under
review
Underground: Hounslow West
then bus A1 (express), 82
Bus: 81, 140, 223, 285

Herne Hill Cycle Track
Burbage Road, SE24
Underground: Brixton then
bus 37
Bus: 2, 2A, 3, 40, 40A, 68, 172,
196 to Herne Hill station then
short walk

Highgate Cemetery
Swains Lane, N6
Underground: Archway
Bus: 210, 271, C11

Highgate Village N6
Underground: Archway then
bus 210, 271

Hogarth's House
Hogarth Lane, Chiswick, W4
Apr to Sept, Mons to Sats
(including Sat & Mon at Easter
& Spring & Late Summer
Hol Mons) 11 00 to 18 00,
Suns (including Easter Sun)
14 00 to 18 00. Oct to Mar,
Mons to Sats (except Tues)
11 00 to 16 00, Suns 14 00 to
16 00. Closed Good Fri,
Christmas Eve
Boxing Day. 5p, children 3p
Underground: Hammersmith
then bus 290

Holland Park
Holland Walk, W8
Underground: Holland Park
Bus: 9, 9A, 12, 27, 28, 31, 33,
49, 73, 88

Honourable Artillery Company
Armoury House, City Road,
EC1

Underground: Moorgate,
Old Street
Bus: 21, 43, 76, 104, 141, 214,
271

Horniman Museum
(and Library) London Road,
Forest Hill, SE23 3PQ
Mons to Sats 10 30 to 18 00
Suns 14 00 to 18 00. Closed
Christmas Eve & Day
Open Good Fri, Easter
weekend & Mon, Spring &
Late Summer Hol Mons,
Boxing Day. Free
British Rail: Forest Hill
Bus: 12, 12A, 63, 176, 176A, 185

Horse Guards Whitehall, SW1
Underground: Charing Cross,
Trafalgar Square, Strand
Bus: 3, 11, 12, 24, 29, 39, 53,
59, 76, 77, 77A, 77B, 77C, 88,
159, 168, 168B, 170

Horticultural Halls
Greycoat Street and Vincent
Square, SW1
Underground: St James's Park,
Victoria
Bus: 2, 2B, 10, 11, 24, 26, 29,
36, 36A, 36B, 39, 149, 181, 185,
503, 507

House of St Barnabas-in-Soho
1 Greek Street, Soho Square,
W1V 6NQ
Mons (except Easter Mon,
Spring & Late Summer Hol
Mons, Christmas Day)
10 30 to 12 00, Thurs
14 30 to 16 15. Special
arrangements for parties.
Free (collecting box at door)
Underground: Tottenham Court
Road
Bus: 1, 7, 8, 14, 19, 22, 24, 25,
29, 38, 73, 176

Houses of Parliament
Parliament Square, SW1
When neither House is sitting:
Sats (including Sat at Easter),
Easter Mon & Tues, Spring
Hol Mon, Mons, Tues & Thurs
in Aug (including Late Summer
Hol Mon) & Thurs in Sept
10 00 to 17 00 (last admission
16 30); conducted tours Sats,
& on other days if guides
available. *During sessions:*
admission to Strangers' Gallery
in either House by advance
application to a MP or
(for Lords) a Peer; or by
queuing at St Stephen's
Entrance. Head of queue for
Lords admitted from about
14 40 Mons, Tues, Weds
& 1510 Thurs; for Commons,
from about 1615 Mons to
Thurs, 11 30 Fris (expect a long
wait during important debates)

WESTMINSTER HALL
When Parliament is in session:
Mons to Thurs 10 00 to 13 30
(if neither House is sitting at
the time), Sats 10 00 to 17 00
During recess: Mons to Fris
10 00 to 16 00, Sats 10 00 to
17 00. Closed Good Fri,
Christmas Day, Boxing Day
Underground: Westminster
Bus: 3, 11, 12, 24, 29, 39, 53,
59, 76, 77, 77A, 77B, 77C,
88, 109, 155, 159, 168, 168B,
170, 172, 184, 503

Hurlingham Park
Fulham, SW6
Underground: Putney Bridge
Bus: 14, 22, 30, 74, 85, 85A,
93, 220

Hyde Park Corner W1
Underground: Hyde Park
Corner
Bus: 2, 2B, 9, 9A, 14, 16, 19,

22, 25, 26, 30, 36, 36A, 36B,
38, 52, 73, 74, 74B, 137, 500

Imperial War Museum
Lambeth Road, SE1
Mons to Sats 10 00 to 18 00
Suns 14 00 to 18 00
Closed Good Fri, Christmas
Eve & Day, Boxing Day. Open
Easter weekend & Mon,
Spring & Late Summer Hol
Mons. 10p (20p July & Aug),
pensioners & children 15 &
under 5p
Underground: Lambeth North,
Elephant & Castle
Bus: 3, 10A, 44, 59, 109, 155,
159, 172

India House Aldwych, WC2
LIBRARY Mons to Fris 09 45 to
18 00. Closed 26 Jan, Good Fri,
Easter Mon, Spring & Late
Summer Hol Mons, 15 Aug,
2 Oct, Christmas Day,
Boxing Day. Free
Underground: Temple
Bus: 1, 1A, 4, 6, 9, 9A, 11, 13,
15, 55, 68, 77, 77A, 170, 171,
172, 176, 188, 196, 239, 502, 505,
513

**Industrial Health and
Safety Centre**
97 Horseferry Road, SW1P 2DY
Mons to Fris 10 00 to 16 30
Closed Good Fri, Easter Mon,
Spring & Late Summer Hol
Mons, Christmas Day, Boxing
Day. Free
Underground: St James's Park
Bus: 11, 24, 29, 39, 503 to
Strutton Ground; 10, 88, 149,
507 to Horseferry Road

Institute of Contemporary Arts
Nash House, The Mall, SW1
Tues to Sats including Sat at
Easter 12 00 to 20 00, Suns
including Easter Sun 14 00 to

22 00. Closed Good Fri,
Christmas Day, Boxing Day
Admission charges vary with
exhibitions
Underground: Trafalgar Square,
Piccadilly Circus
Bus: see *National Gallery*

Iveagh Bequest
see *Kenwood House*

Jewel Tower
Old Palace Yard, SW1
Mons to Sats 10 30 to 16 00
Open Good Fri, Sat & Mon at
Easter, Spring & Late Summer
Hol Mons. Closed Christmas
Eve & Day, Boxing Day. Free
see *Houses of Parliament*

Jewish Museum
Woburn House,
Upper Woburn Place, WC1
Mons to Thurs 14 30 to 17 00
Fris & Suns 10 30 to 12 45
Special arrangements can be
made for parties
Closed Sats, Jewish Holy Days,
Good Fri, Easter Mon,
Spring & Late Summer Hol
Mons, Christmas Day,
Boxing Day. Open Christmas
Eve. Free
Underground: Euston,
Euston Square, Russell Square
Bus: 14, 18, 30, 68, 73, 77, 77A,
77B, 77C, 170, 188, 196, 239

Dr Johnson's House
17 Gough Square, EC4A 3DE
Mons to Sats, May to Sept
10 30 to 17 00, Oct to Apr
(including Sat at Easter)
10 30 to 16 30. Closed
Good Fri, Easter Mon,
Spring & Late Summer Hol
Mons, Christmas Day, Boxing
Day. 10p, students &
children 5p
see *St Bride's Church*

Keats House Keats Grove,
Hampstead, NW3
Tel: 01-435 2062
Mons to Sats 10 00 to 18 00
(Easter Mon & Spring & Late
Summer Hol Mons 10 00 to
13 00 & 14 00 to 18 00). Closed
Good Fri, Sat at Easter,
Christmas Day, Boxing Day.
Free
Underground: Belsize Park,
Hampstead
Bus: 24, 46, 187, 268, C11

Kempton Park
Sunbury-on-Thames, Middlesex
British Rail: Kempton Park
(race days only)
Bus: 90, 216, 237, 264

Kensington Gardens W2 & W8
Underground: Queensway,
High Street Kensington,
Lancaster Gate
Bus: 9, 9A, 12, 27, 28, 31, 33,
49, 52, 73, 88

Kensington Palace
Kensington Gardens, W8
see *London Museum*

Kenwood House
Hampstead Lane, NW3
Mons to Sats 10 00 to 19 00
Suns 14 00 to 19 00
Closes 17 00 Oct, Feb, March;
16 00 Nov to Jan
Closed Good Fri, Christmas
Eve & Day. Open Sat, Sun &
Mon at Easter, Spring & Late
Summer Hol Mons, Boxing Day
15p, children 5p on Mons &
Sats; other days free.
Park daily 08 00 to dusk. Free
Underground: Archway or
Golders Green then bus 210

**Kew Gardens, Palace and
Queen's Cottage** Kew, Surrey
GARDENS daily (except

Christmas Day) 10 00 to 20 00 or
an hour before sunset if earlier
Admission charge under review

HOUSES daily (except
Christmas Day) 13 00 to
16 50 (17 50 on Suns) or
dusk if earlier. Admission
charges under consideration

MUSEUMS daily (except
Good Fri, Christmas Eve &
Day, Boxing Day) 10 00 to
16 50 (17 50 on Suns) or
dusk if earlier. Admission
charges under consideration

PALACE Apr to Sept, Mons to
Sats 11 00 to 17 30, Suns
14 00 to 18 00. Open Good Fri
(hours as for Apr), Easter
weekend & Mon, Spring &
Late Summer Hol Mons. 5p,
children & pensioners 2½p

COTTAGE Apr to Sept, Sats &
Suns (including Easter
weekend), Easter Mon,
Spring & Late Summer Hol
Mons 14 00 to 18 00. Free
Underground: Kew Gardens
Bus: 15, 27, 65, 90, 90B

King's College Strand, WC2
see *Australia House*

King's Cross BR Station N1
Underground: King's Cross
Bus: 14, 17, 18, 30, 45, 46, 63, 73,
77A, 77B, 77C, 168A, 214, 221,
239, 259, 263

Kingston-upon-Thames
Underground: Richmond then
bus 65, 71 or Wimbledon then
bus 57, 131, 155

Lambeth Palace
Lambeth Road, SE1
Sometimes open to public for
charity—see details in press

Underground: Westminster
then bus 3, 77, 77A, 77C, 159,
168, 168B, 170
Bus: 10A, 44, 149, 168A, 507

Lancaster House Stable Yard,
St James's Palace, SW1
Easter Eve to mid-Dec
Sats, Suns, Easter Mon &
Spring & Late Summer Hol
Mons 14 00 to 18 00. 15p
children under 15 & pensioners
5p
Closed at short notice if needed
for Government functions
Underground: Green Park
Bus: 9, 9A, 14, 19, 22, 25, 38, 506

Law Courts Strand, WC2
The public galleries are usually
open during legal terms: Mons
to Fris 10 30 to 13 00 &
14 00 to 16 00
Underground: Temple
Bus: 1, 4, 6, 9, 9A, 11, 13, 15,
68, 77, 77A, 170, 171, 172, 176,
188, 196, 239, 502, 505, 513

Leadenhall Market
Gracechurch Street, EC3
Underground: Bank, Monument
Bus: 8A, 10, 15, 25, 35, 40, 47,
48

Leather Lane Market
Leather Lane, EC1
Mons to Fris 11 00 to 15 00
Underground: Chancery Lane
Bus: 5, 8, 17, 18, 22, 25, 45, 46,
55, 171, 243, 259, 501

Lee Valley Regional Park
THREE MILLS CENTRE
Three Mill Lane, Bromley-
by-Bow, E3
and
Bisson Road, E15
Mons to Fris 09 00 to 23 00
Sats 09 00 to 17 00

Closed Good Fri, Sat and
Mon at Easter, Spring & Late
Summer Hol Mons, Christmas
Eve & Day, Boxing Day.
Admission free, football
pitch charges vary
For Three Mill Lane
Underground: Bromley-by-Bow
Bus: 86, 108, S2
For Bisson Road
Underground: Stratford
Bus: 10, 25, 86

LEA BRIDGE RIDING SCHOOL
Lea Bridge Road, E5
Tues to Suns 09 30 to 20 30
Closed Christmas Day,
Boxing Day
Open Good Fri, Sat & Mon
at Easter, Spring & Late
Summer Hol Mons, Christmas
Eve 09 30 to 18 30. Charges
on application
British Rail: Lea Bridge
Bus: 38, 48, 55, 256

SPRINGFIELD MARINA
Springhill, E5
Mons to Fris 09 30 to 17 30
Sats and Suns 09 30 to 12 00
Closed Good Fri, Sat to Mon
at Easter, Spring & Late
Summer Hol Mons, Christmas
Eve & Day, Boxing Day
Admission free, mooring fees
on application
British Rail: Stamford Hill
then bus 253
Bus: 67, 76, 97, 149, 243,
243A to Stamford Hill

MARKFIELD BEAM ENGINE
Markfield Road, Haringey, N22
Admission only by prior
arrangement with the Lee
Valley Regional Park
Authority (Tel: Waltham Cross
20711)
Underground: Seven Sisters,
Tottenham Hale
Bus: 41, 123, 241

27

Walthamstow Avenue, North
Circular Road, E4
Mons to Sats 09 30 to dusk
Suns 09 30 to 17 00 or dusk if
earlier
Closed Good Fri, Sat to Mon
at Easter, Christmas Day,
Boxing Day. Open Spring and
Late Summer Hol Mons,
Christmas Eve. Admission
free, instructional charges on
application
British Rail: Angel Road, then
bus 34, 144
Bus: 58, 256

PICKETTS LOCK CENTRE
Picketts Lock Lane,
Edmonton, N9
Opens March 1973
daily except Christmas Day.
10p, children 5p
Mons to Fris 10 00 to 23 00
(24 00 on Fris), Sats and Suns
09 00 to 23 00 (24 00 on Sats)
British Rail: Lower Edmonton
Bus: 76, 149, 191, 279

KING GEORGE'S SAILING CLUB
Lea Valley Road, E4
Tues to Thurs 14 00 to dusk
Sats and Suns 09 30 to dusk
Closed Christmas Eve & Day,
Boxing Day. Open Good Fri,
Sat to Mon at Easter, Spring
& Late Summer Hol Mons
Admission to club members
only
British Rail: Ponders End
Bus: 121, 242, 276

Leicester Square WC2
Underground: Leicester Square
Bus: 1, 24, 29, 176

Leighton House
12 Holland Park Road,
W14 8LZ
Mons to Sats 11 00 to 17 00
(Mons to Fris to 18 00 during

exhibitions). Closed Good Fri,
Sat & Mon at Easter, Spring &
Late Summer Hol Mons,
Christmas Day, Boxing Day
Free (special charges sometimes
made for temporary
exhibitions in parts of the
house only)
Underground: High Street
Kensington
Bus: 9, 9A, 27, 28, 33, 49, 73

Lincoln's Inn
Chancery Lane, WC2
Visitors please call at porter's
lodge on way in
HALLS, LIBRARY AND CHAPEL
Mons to Fris 10 00 to 16 30

GARDENS
Mons to Fris 12 00 to 14 30
Closed Good Fri, Easter Mon,
Spring & Late Summer
Hol Mons, Christmas Day,
Boxing Day. Free
Underground: Chancery Lane
Bus: 8, 22, 25, 171, 501

Lincoln's Inn Fields WC2
Underground· Holborn
Bus: 8, 22, 25, 55, 68, 77, 77A,
77B, 77C, 170, 172, 188, 196,
239, 501

Little Stanmore Church
Whitchurch Lane, Edgware,
Middlesex
Underground: Canons Park
Bus: 79A, 186, 286

Little Venice (Regent's Canal)
Paddington, W2
Summer waterbuses to and
from the Zoo (and round trips)
late Mar to early Oct
Tel: 01-286 6101
Underground: Warwick Avenue
Bus: 6, 8, 16, 18, 187, 616

Liverpool Street BR Station EC2
Underground: Liverpool Street
Bus: 6, 8, 8A, 9, 11, 22, 35, 47,
48, 78, 97, 133, 149, 243A, 502

Lloyd's Leadenhall Street, EC3
Underground: Bank, Monument
Bus: 15, 25

London Bridge BR Station SE1
Underground: London Bridge
Bus: 8A, 10, 10A, 18, 21, 35,
40, 40A, 43, 44, 47, 48, 70,
133, 501, 513

London Hospital
Whitechapel Road, E1
Underground: Whitechapel
Bus: 10, 25, 253

**London Museum, State
Apartments and Orangery**
Kensington Palace, The Broad
Walk, Kensington Gardens, W8
Mar to Sept Mons to Sats
10 00 to 18 00, Suns 14 00 to
18 00. Oct & Feb Mons to Sats
10 00 to 17 00, Suns 14 00 to
17 00. Nov, Dec, Jan Mons
to Sats 10 00 to 16 00, Suns
14 00 to 16 00. Closed Good Fri,
Christmas Eve & Day, Boxing
Day. Open Easter weekend &
Mon, Spring & Late Summer
Hol Mons. 10p (July & Aug
20p), children 15 & under &
pensioners 5p
Underground: Queensway, High
Street Kensington
Bus: 9, 9A, 12, 27, 28, 31, 33,
49, 52, 73, 88

London School of Economics
Houghton Street, Aldwych,
WC2
see *Australia House*

London Silver Vaults
Chancery House,
Chancery Lane, WC2
Mons to Fris 09 00 to 17 30

Sats 09 00 to 12 30
Closed Good Fri, Sat & Mon
at Easter, Spring & Late
Summer Hol Mons,
Christmas Day, Boxing Day.
No admission charge
Underground: Chancery Lane
Bus: 8, 22, 25, 171, 501

London Stone Bank of China,
Cannon Street, EC4
Underground: Cannon Street,
Monument
Bus: 9A, 18, 95, 149, 176A, 513

London's Wall
TOWER OF LONDON, EC3
WAKEFIELD GARDENS, EC3
PLATFORM 1, TOWER HILL
UNDERGROUND STATION
COOPER'S ROW, EC3
Underground: Tower Hill
Bus: 9A, 42, 78

CAR PARK, south of St Giles
Cripplegate
Roman Fort's West Gateway
Mons to Fris 12 30 to 14 30 and
at other times by arrangement
with the Director of the
Guildhall Museum. Closed
Good Fri, Easter Mon, Spring
& Late Summer Hol Mons,
Christmas Day, Boxing Day
Free

ST ALPHAGE GARDEN, London
Wall, EC2

ST GILES CRIPPLEGATE, EC1
NOBLE STREET, EC2
Underground: Barbican,
Moorgate, St Paul's
Bus: 4, 141, 502

KING EDWARD BUILDING,
POST OFFICE, EC1A 1AA
see *Post Office*

ALL HALLOWS-ON-THE-WALL
CHURCH, London Wall, EC2
Underground: Liverpool Street
Bus: 11, 133, 502

London Tourist Board

ENQUIRY OFFICES

4 Grosvenor Gardens,
Victoria, SW1W 0DU
Mons to Fris 09 15 to 17 30
see *Victoria BR Station*

Victoria BR Station (platform
15). Daily 09 00 to 21 00 (winter),
07 30 to 23 00 (summer)
see *Victoria BR Station*

BOAC Air Terminal,
Buckingham Palace Road, SW1
Summer months only, daily
09 00 to 14 00
see *Air Terminals—BOAC*

STUDENT CENTRE
8-10 Buckingham Palace Road,
Victoria, SW1
Daily 08 00 to 23 00 (Summer),
Mons to Fris 09 15 to 17 30
(Winter)

TELEPHONE ENQUIRIES
TOURIST INFORMATION 01-730
0791 daily 09 00 to 18 00
(winter), 08 00 to 20 00
(summer)

HOTEL BOOKINGS 01-730 9845
Daily 08 00 to 23 00 (Summer),
09 00 to 19 00 (Winter)

DAILY EVENTS DIARY
01-246 8041 (English)
  8043 (French)
  8045 (German)
  8047 (Spanish)
  8049 (Italian)
  any time

London Transport

ENQUIRY OFFICES AT
UNDERGROUND STATIONS
Open daily except Christmas
Day 08 30 to 21 30 at
Euston, King's Cross, Oxford
Circus, Piccadilly Circus,
St James's Park & Victoria

ENQUIRIES BY TELEPHONE
01-222 1234
any time day or night

LOST PROPERTY OFFICE
200 Baker Street, NW1
Mons to Fris 10 00 to 18 00
Closed Good Fri, Easter Mon,
Spring & Late Summer Hol
Mons, Christmas Day,
Boxing Day
Underground: Baker Street
Bus: see *Madame Tussaud's*

PUBLICITY POSTER SHOP
Griffith House, 280 Old
Marylebone Road, NW1 5RJ
Mons to Thurs 09 00 to 16 30
Fris 09 00 to 16 00
Closed Good Fri, Easter Mon
Spring & Late Summer Hol
Mons, Christmas Day,
Boxing Day
Underground: Edgware Road
(Metropolitan Line)
Bus: 6, 7, 8, 15, 16, 18, 27, 36,
36A, 36B, 176, 616

London Zoo

Regent's Park, NW1 4RY
Daily except Christmas Day
Mar to Oct 09 00 to 18 00
(Suns & Easter Mon & Spring
& Late Summer Hol Mons to
19 00), Nov to Feb 10 00 to 17 00
or sunset if earlier. 50p,
children 14 & under 30p (Mons
except public hols 40p, 20p),
students 20p, pensioners 10p

AQUARIUM 10p, children 5p

CHILDREN'S ZOO Mar to Oct
Mons to Sats 10 3 0 to 17 30,
Suns & Easter Mon & Spring
& Late Summer Hol Mons
10 30 to 18 15; Nov to Feb
10 30 to 16 00, Suns & Boxing
Day 10 30 to 15 30
10p children 5p
All charges under review
Underground: Camden Town or
Baker Street then bus 74, 74B
Bus: 3, 53

Lord's Cricket Ground
see *Cricket*

The Mall SW1
Underground: Trafalgar Square,
St James's Park, Green Park
Bus: 1, 1A, 3, 6, 9, 9A, 11, 12,
13, 14, 15, 19, 22, 24, 29, 38,
39, 53, 59, 77, 77A, 77B, 77C,
88, 159, 168, 168B, 170, 176,
505, 506

Mall Gallery The Mall, SW1
Times vary with exhibitions
(closed between exhibitions)
20p, students, pensioners &
children 10 & under 10p
Some exhibitions in east
gallery free
Underground: Trafalgar Square,
Piccadilly Circus
Bus: see National Gallery

Manor House Hospital
North End Road, NW11
Underground: Golders Green
then bus 210, 268

Mansion House
Mansion House Street,
EC4N 8BH
Admission on certain Sats
only on prior written application
to Lord Mayor
Underground: Bank
Bus: 6, 8, 9, 9A, 11, 15, 21,
22, 25, 43, 76, 133, 149, 501,
502

Marble Arch W1
Underground: Marble Arch
Bus: 2, 2B, 6, 7, 8, 12, 15, 16,
26, 30, 36, 36A, 36B, 73, 74,
74B, 88, 137, 500, 505, 616

Marble Hill House and Park
Richmond Road,
Twickenham, Middlesex
HOUSE Tues to Sats
(including Sat at Easter) &
Easter Mon, Spring & Late
Summer Hol Mons, Boxing Day
10 00 to 17 00, Suns (including

Easter Sun) 14 00 to 17 00
Closed Good Fri, Christmas
Eve & Day. 10p, children 5p
PARK daily, free
Underground: Richmond then
bus 27, 33, 73, 90, 90B, 202,
270

**Marlborough House and
Queen's Chapel**
Marlborough Road,
Pall Mall, SW1
Visits to House and Chapel
may be arranged by applying to
the Administration Officer
Tel: 01-930 9249

CHAPEL Mons to Fris only
HOUSE Easter to Sept Sats, Suns
(including Easter weekend)
& Easter Mon & Spring & Late
Summer Hol Mons 14 00 to
18 00. 5p, children 16 &
under 3p

COMMONWEALTH INFORMATION
CENTRE and READING ROOM
Mons to Fris 10 00 to 16 30
Closed Good Fri, Easter Mon,
Spring & Late Summer Hol
Mons, Christmas Day,
Boxing Day. Free
House and Centre may be
closed at short notice for
conferences
see St James's Palace

Marylebone BR Station NW1
Underground: Marylebone
Bus: 1, 18, 27, 176

Middlesex Guildhall
Broad Sanctuary, SW1
The public are admitted when
the Courts are sitting
see Houses of Parliament

Middlesex Hospital
Mortimer Street, W1
Underground: Goodge Street,
Oxford Circus
Bus: see Building Centre

Mitcham Common
Mitcham, Surrey
Underground: Tooting
Broadway then bus 44, 64, 77,
88, 280
Bus: 115, 115A, 118

Monument
Fish Street Hill, EC3
Mons to Sats Apr to Sept
09 00 to 17 40, Oct to Mar
09 00 to 15 40; Suns May to
Sept 14 00 to 17 40. Closed
Good Fri, Christmas Day,
Boxing Day. Open Sat & Mon
at Easter, Spring & Late
Summer Hol Mons. 5p,
children 14 & under 2½p
Underground: Monument
Bus: 8A, 9A, 10, 21, 35, 40,
40A, 43, 44, 47, 48, 133, 501, 513

Moorfields Eye Hospital
City Road, EC1
Underground: Old Street
Bus: 5, 43, 55, 76, 104, 141,
214, 243, 271

Morden College
Blackheath, SE3 0PW
To view write to the
Clerk of the Trustees
British Rail: Blackheath
Bus: 53, 54, 75, 89, 108, 108B,
192

Morley College 61 Westminster
Bridge Road, SE1
Underground: Lambeth North
Bus: 12, 53, 171, 184

**Museum for Historical
Instruments**
see *Royal College of Music*

National Army Museum
Royal Hospital Road,
Chelsea, SW3 4HT
Mons to Sats (including

Sat at Easter, Easter Mon,
Spring & Late Summer Hol
Mons) 10 00 to 17 30; Suns
(including Easter Sun) 14 00
to 17 30. Closed Good Fri,
Christmas Eve & Day,
Boxing Day. Admission
charges under consideration
see *Chelsea Royal Hospital*

National Book League
7 Albemarle Street, W1X 4BB
Mons to Fris 09 30 to 21 00
(exhibitions 10 00 to 18 00),
Sats 10 00 to 13 00
Closed Good Fri, Easter Mon,
Spring & Late Summer Hol
Mons, Christmas Day,
Boxing Day. Usually free
Underground: Green Park
Bus: 9, 14, 19, 22, 25, 38, 506

National Gallery
Trafalgar Square, WC2N 5DN
Mons to Sats (including Sat &
Mon at Easter, Spring & Late
Summer Hol Mons) 10 00 to
18 00 (Tues & Thurs to 21 00
June to Sept); Suns (including
Easter Sun) & Boxing Day
14 00 to 18 00. Closed
Christmas Eve & Day
Admission charges under
consideration
Underground: Strand,
Trafalgar Square
Bus: 1, 1A, 3, 6, 9, 9A, 11, 12,
13, 15, 24, 29, 39, 53, 59, 77,
77A, 77B, 77C, 88, 159, 168,
168B, 170, 176, 505

National Institute for the Blind
224 Great Portland Street, W1
Underground: Regent's Park,
Great Portland Street
Bus: 3, 53, 137

**National Maritime Museum
including Queen's House**
see *Greenwich*

National Portrait Gallery
St Martin's Place, Trafalgar
Square, WC2H 0HE
Mons to Fris 10 00 to 17 00
Sats 10 00 to 18 00
Suns 14 00 to 18 00
Closed Good Fri, Christmas
Eve & Day. Open Sat, Sun &
Mon at Easter & Spring & Late
Summer Hol Mons. Boxing
Day plans under review. 10p
(July & Aug 20p), pensioners
& children 15 & under 5p
Season ticket £1, pensioners
& children 50p
Underground: Leicester Square,
Trafalgar Square
Bus: see *National Gallery*

National Postal Museum
London Chief Office,
King Edward Street, EC1A 1LP
Mons to Fris 10 00 to 16 30
Sats 10 00 to 16 00. Closed
Good Fri, Sat & Mon at
Easter, Spring & Late Summer
Hol Mons, Christmas Day,
Boxing Day. Free
Special arrangements
for parties. Tel: 01-432 3851
Underground: St Paul's
Bus: 4, 8, 22, 25, 141, 501, 502

Natural History Museum
Cromwell Road,
South Kensington, SW7 5BD
Mons to Sats 10 00 to 18 00
Suns 14 30 to 18 00. Closed
Good Fri, Christmas Eve &
Day, Boxing Day. Open
Easter weekend & Mon,
Spring & Late Summer Hol
Mons. Admission charges
under consideration
see *Science Museum*

New Zealand House
Haymarket, SW1
REFERENCE LIBRARY
Mons to Fris 09 00 to 17 00

CINEMA Weds 14 00 & 15 15
Closed New Year's Day,
Good Fri, Easter Mon,
25 Apr, Spring & Late
Summer Hol Mons,
Christmas Day, Boxing Day
Free
Underground: Piccadilly Circus
Bus: see *National Gallery*

Northwick Park Hospital
near Harrow, Middlesex
Underground or British Rail:
Kenton
Underground: Northwick Park
Bus: 140, 182, 183

Olave House
(Girl Guide Hostel)
45 Longridge Road, SW5
Underground: Earl's Court
Bus: 31, 74, 74B

Old Bailey
(Central Criminal Court)
Old Bailey, EC4 7BS
The public are admitted when
the Courts are sitting
Underground: St Paul's
Bus: 4, 6, 8, 9, 9A, 11, 15, 18,
22, 25, 141, 501, 502, 513

Old Curiosity Shop
Portsmouth Street,
Kingsway, WC2
Daily except Christmas Day
09 30 to 17 30 (from 09 00
April to Oct). No admission
charge
Underground: Holborn
Bus: 55, 68, 77, 77A, 77B, 77C,
170, 172, 188, 196, 239

Old Royal Observatory
see *Greenwich*

Olympia
Hammersmith Road, W14
Underground: Kensington
(Olympia)
Bus: 9, 9A, 27, 28, 33, 49, 73, 91

Operating Theatre (Old St
Thomas's Hospital) Southwark
Cathedral Chapter House,
St Thomas's Street, SE1
Mons, Weds, Fris 12 30 to 16 00
Closed Good Fri, Easter Mon,
Spring & Late Summer Hol
Mons, Christmas Day. 20p,
children 14 & under 10p,
students 7½p
Underground: London Bridge
Bus: 8A, 10, 10A, 18, 21, 35,
40, 40A, 43, 44, 47, 48, 70,
133, 501, 513

Orleans House Gallery
Riverside, Twickenham
Tues to Sats 13 00 to 17 30 (to
16 30 Oct to Mar), Suns 14 00
to 17 30 (16 30 Oct to Mar).
Easter Mon, Spring & Late
Summer Hol Mons 14 00 to
17 30. Closed Good Fri,
Christmas Day,
Boxing Day. Free
Underground or British Rail:
Richmond then bus 27, 90,
90B, 202, 270
Bus: 33, 73

Orpington Museum The Priory,
Church Hill, Orpington,
Kent, BR6 0HH
Mons to Fris (except Thurs)
09 00 to 18 00, Sats (including
Sat at Easter) 09 00 to 17 00
Closed Good Fri, Easter Mon,
Spring & Late Summer Hol
Mons, Christmas Day,
Boxing Day. Free
British Rail: Orpington
Bus: 51, 51A, 61, 94, 229

Osterley Park
Osterley, Middlesex
HOUSE Tues to Suns (including
Easter weekend) & Easter Mon]
& Spring & Late Summer Hol
Mons: Apr to Sept 14 00 to
18 00, Oct to Mar 12 00 to 16 00

Closed Good Fri, Christmas
Day, Boxing Day. 20p,
pensioners and children 10p
Unaccompanied children under
12 not admitted
PARK daily throughout year
10 00 to dusk. Free
Underground: Osterley
Bus: 91, 116

Oval Cricket Ground
see *Cricket*

Paddington BR Station W2
Underground: Paddington
Bus: 7, 15, 27, 36, 36A, 36B

Passmore Edwards Museum
Romford Road, Stratford, E15
Mons to Fris 10 00 to 18 00,
(Thurs to 20 00), Sats 10 00 to
13 00 & 14 00 to 17 00. Closed
Good Fri, Sat & Mon at
Easter, Spring & Late Summer
Hol Mons, Christmas Eve &
Day, Boxing Day. Free
Underground: Stratford
Bus: 25, 86, 169A, S3;
10, 238, 241, 262, S1 to
Stratford Broadway

Passport Office Clive House,
Petty France, SW1H 9HD
Mons to Fris 09 00 to 16 30
Closed Good Fri, Easter Mon,
Spring & Late Summer Hol
Mons, Christmas Day,
Boxing Day
Underground: St James's Park
Bus: 10, 11, 24, 29, 39, 149,
503, 507

Pepys Estate Grove Street, SE8
Underground: Surrey Docks
Bus: 1, 1A, 47, 70, 108B

**Percival David Foundation of
Chinese Art**
53 Gordon Square, WC1H 0PD
Mons 14 00 to 17 00, Tues to

Fris 10 30 to 17 00, Sats
10 30 to 13 00. Closed Good Fri,
Sat & Mon at Easter, Spring &
Late Summer Hol Mons
& preceding Sats, Christmas
Day, Boxing Day. Free
see *Courtauld Institute Galleries*

Petticoat Lane Market
Middlesex Street, E1
Sunday mornings
Underground: Liverpool Street,
Aldgate, Aldgate East
Bus: 5, 6, 8, 9A, 10, 15, 22, 23,
25, 35, 40, 42, 44, 47, 48, 67,
78, 95, 149, 243A, 253

Piccadilly Circus W1
Underground: Piccadilly Circus
Bus: 3, 6, 9, 9A, 12, 13, 14, 15,
19, 22, 38, 39, 53, 59, 88, 159,
505, 506

Pitshanger Manor
Ealing Public Library,
Walpole Park, Ealing, W5
Underground: Ealing Broadway
Bus: 65, 83, 112, 207, 273,
274, E1, E2

Planetarium
Marylebone Road, NW1 5LR
Presentations every hour on the
hour (more frequently in July
& Aug): Apr to Sept daily
(including Easter weekend
& Mon, Spring & Late
Summer Hol Mons) 11 00 to
18 00; Oct to Mar Mons to Fris
11 00 to 17 00 (Christmas Eve to
16 00 only), Sats & Suns &
Good Fri 11 00 to 18 00.
Boxing Day 12 00 to 18 00.
Closed Christmas Day. 30p
(from 1 April 35p), pensioners
& children 13 & under 15p
(from 1 April 20p)
(under-fives not admitted)
Royal ticket including Madame
Tussaud's 75p, children 35p
(from 1 April 85p and 40p)
see *Madame Tussaud's*

Pollock's Toy Museum
1 Scala Street, W1
Mons to Sats 10 00 to 17 00
Closed Good Fri, Easter Mon,
Spring & Late Summer Hol
Mons, Christmas Day,
Boxing Day. 10p, children 5p
Underground: Goodge Street
Bus: 14, 24, 29, 73, 176

Polytechnic of Central London
Regent Street, W1
see *Broadcasting House*

Port of London
Public Relations Officer
Port of London Authority,
World Trade Centre,
London, E1
Underground: Aldgate, Aldgate
East
Bus: 9A, 42, 67, 78

INDIA & MILLWALL DOCKS
Underground: Mile End then
bus 106, 277
Bus: 5, 15, 23, 40, 40A, 86

VICTORIA, ALBERT AND
KING GEORGE V DOCKS
Underground: Plaistow then
bus 69, 241, 262 or
East Ham then bus 101
Bus: 278

Portobello Market
Portobello Road, W10
Sats mainly
Underground: Ladbroke Grove,
Notting Hill Gate
Bus: 7, 15, 52

Postmen's Park
Aldersgate Street, EC1
see *Post Office—King Edward
Building*

Post Office
To view apply to the addresses
below, giving as much notice
as possible

Children under 14 are not
normally admitted unless
accompanied by adults
Tours take from 1 to 2 hours

(Parties limited to 13)
Mons to Weds at 15 00
The Manager, London Inland
Telegraphs, LIT/AB, Fleet
Building, 40 Shoe Lane,
EC4A 3DD. Tel: 01-829 3750
see *Post Office—King Edward
Building*

ELECTRA HOUSE
(Parties limited to 15)
Mons to Thurs 10 15, 14 15, 19 15
Times will be given by letter
Telegraph Manager,
Commercial Division,
Electra House, Victoria
Embankment, WC2R 3HL
Tel: 01-836 1222, Ext. 2663
Underground: Temple
Bus: 109, 155, 168, 172, 184

FARADAY BUILDING
Trunk, Continental and
International Exchange,
Queen Victoria Street,
EC4V 4BU
Mons to Fris 10 00 to 12 00,
14 00 to 16 00 and 18 00 to 20 00
(parties limited to 25)
Sats 18 00 & 18 30 only
(parties limited to 15)
General Manager, Iternation
Telephone Services, GMITp/
SG113, Faraday Building,
Queen Victoria Street,
EC4V 4BU
Tel: 01-248 4174
Underground: Blackfriars
Bus: 17, 45, 63, 76, 109, 141
155, 168A, 184

KING EDWARD BUILDING
King Edward Street, EC1A 1AA
(Parties limited to 20)
Mons to Thurs 10 00 to 19 30
(organized parties of

schoolchildren), 16 00 to 19 30
(organized parties of adults)
The Postmaster Controller
(S & B Branch)
Tel: 01-432 3176
Underground: St Paul's
Bus: 4, 8, 22, 25, 141, 501

POSTAL MUSEUM
see *National Postal Museum*

Post Office Tower
Maple Street, W1P 5FR
Tel: 01-636 3133

VIEWING GALLERIES
Closed until further notice
Underground: Warren Street,
Great Portland Street
Bus: 14, 18, 24, 27, 29, 30, 73,
134, 137, 176, 253

Prince Henry's Room
17 Fleet Street, EC4
Mons to Fris 13 45 to 17 00,
Sats 13 45 to 16 30. Closed
Good Fri, Sat & Mon at
Easter, Spring & Late Summer
Hol Mons, Christmas Day,
Boxing Day. Free
Underground: Temple
Bus: 4, 6, 9, 9A, 11, 15, 171,
502, 513

**Public Record Office and
Museum**
Chancery Lane, WC2A 1LR
OFFICE Search Rooms (open to
holders of Readers' Tickets
only) Mons to Fris 09 30 to
17 00, Sats 09 30 to 13 00
Closed Good Fri, Sat & Mon
at Easter, 25 May, Spring &
Late Summer Hol Mons,
Christmas Day, Boxing Day
Free

MUSEUM Mons to Fris 13 00 to
16 00, organized parties at other
times by arrangement
Closed Good Fri, Easter Mon.
25 May, Spring & Late

Summer Hol Mons, Christmas
Eve & Day, Boxing Day. Free
Underground: Chancery Lane,
Temple
Bus: 4, 6, 9, 11, 15, 171, 502,
513

Purcell Room South Bank SE1
see *Royal Festival Hall*

Queen Anne's Gate
Westminster, SW1
Underground: St James's Park
Bus: 11, 24, 29, 39, 503

**Queen Charlotte's
Maternity Hospital**
339 Goldhawk Road, W6
Underground: Stamford Brook
Bus: 88, 117

Queen Elizabeth Hall
South Bank, SE1
see *Royal Festival Hall*

**Queen Elizabeth's
Hunting Lodge**
Epping Forest Museum,
Rangers Road, Chingford, E4
Weds to Suns (including
Good Fri, Easter weekend &
Mon, Spring & Late Summer
Hol Mons, Christmas Eve)
14 00 to 18 00 or dusk if earlier
5p, children accompanied by
adult free
British Rail: Chingford
Bus: 69, 102, 121, 179, 191,
235, 242, 262 to Chingford
Station, then short walk

Queen Mary's Hospital
Roehampton, SW15
Underground: Hammersmith,
then bus 72 or Putney Bridge
then bus 85, 85A
Bus: 30

Queen's Club
West Kensington, W14
Underground: Barons Court

Bus: 11, 28, 30, 74, 74B, 91,
220, 295

Queen's Gallery
Buckingham Palace,
Buckingham Palace Road, SW1
During exhibitions Tues to
Sats (including Sat at Easter)
& Easter Mon, Spring & Late
Summer Hol Mons 11 00 to
17 00, Suns (including
Easter Sun) 14 00 to 17 00
Christmas plans under review
Closed between exhibitions
15p, children, students &
pensioners 5p
see *Victoria BR Station*

Queen's House
see *Greenwich—National
Maritime Museum*

Queen's Ice Skating Club
Queensway, W2
Underground: Queensway,
Bayswater
Bus: 12, 88

Regent's Park NW1
Underground: Baker Street,
Regent's Park, Great Portland
Street, Camden Town
Bus: 1, 2, 2B, 3, 13, 18, 26, 27,
30, 53, 59, 74, 74B, 113,
137, 159, 176

Richmond Ice Rink
Twickenham, Middlesex
Underground: Richmond
Bus: 27, 33, 37, 73, 90, 90B, 202,
270

Richmond Park Surrey
Underground: Richmond then
bus 65, 71; Putney Bridge then
bus 85
Bus: 33, 37, 72, 73

Richmond-upon-Thames
Underground: Richmond
Bus: 27, 33, 37, 65, 71, 73, 90,
90B, 202, 270, 290

†**Roman Bath**
5 Strand Lane, WC2
Mons to Sats 10 00 to 12 30
Closed Good Fri, Christmas
Day. Open Sat & Mon at
Easter, Spring & Late Summer
Hol Mons, Boxing Day. 5p,
children 2½p
Underground: Temple
Bus: see *Savoy Chapel*

Rotunda Museum
Woolwich Common, SE18 4BJ
Closed until May 1973
Underground: New Cross or
New Cross Gate then bus 53
British Rail: Woolwich
Dockyard
Bus: 53, 54, 75

Round House
Chalk Farm Road, NW1 8BG
Open to view when theatre
activities permit
Mons to Sats 10 00 to 24 00,
Suns (for shows or exhibitions
only) from approx. 15 30,
depending on event. Admission
charges vary
Underground: Chalk Farm
Bus: 24, 31, 68

Royal Academy
Burlington House,
Piccadilly, W1V 0DS
Summer Exhibition (May to
July) & other exhibitions
in course of year. Mons to Sats
10 00 to 18 00 (Thurs to 20 00),
Suns 14 30 to 18 00. Closed only
between exhibitions &
Christmas Day & Boxing Day.
Admission charges vary with
exhibitions (children, students,
pensioners half-price)
Underground: Piccadilly Circus,
Green Park
Bus: 9, 9A, 14, 19, 22, 25, 38,
506

Royal Academy of Music
York Gate,
Marylebone Road, NW1
Underground: Baker Street
Bus: 18, 27, 30, 176

Royal Air Force Museum
Hendon NW9 5LL
Mons to Sats 10 00 to 18 00,
Suns 14 30 to 18 00. Closed
Good Fri, Christmas Day,
Boxing Day. Free
Underground: Colindale
Bus: 79, 266

Royal College of Art
Kensington Gore, SW7
see *Albert Hall*

Royal College of Music
Prince Consort Road, SW7
MUSEUM FOR HISTORICAL
INSTRUMENTS (including
DONALDSON COLLECTION)
By appointment with Curator
only, on Mons & Weds in
term-time 10 00 to 16 00. 10p
Underground: South
Kensington
Bus: 9, 9A, 14, 30, 39A, 45, 49,
52, 73, 74, 74B

Royal Courts of Justice
see *Law Courts*

Royal Exchange Cornhill, EC3
Mons to Fris 10 00 to 16 00
Sats 10 00 to 12 00. Closed
Good Fri, Sat & Mon at Easter,
Spring & Late Summer Hol
Mons, Christmas Day,
Boxing Day. Free
see *Bank of England*

Royal Festival Hall
South Bank, SE1
Underground: Waterloo,
Charing Cross
Bus: 1, 1A, 4, 68, 70, 76, 149,
168A, 171, 176, 188, 196, 239
501, 502, 503, 505, 507, 513

Royal Free Hospital
Gray's Inn Road, WC1
Underground: King's Cross
Bus: 17, 18, 45, 46

Royal Geographical Society
Kensington Gore, SW7
see *Albert Hall*

Royal Institute of British Architects
66 Portland Place, W1
Underground: Regent's Park, Great Portland Street
Bus: 3, 18, 27, 30, 53, 137, 176

HEINZ GALLERY 21 Portman Square, W1
Mons to Fris 11 00 to 17 00
Closed Spring & Late Summer Hol Mons, Christmas Day, Boxing Day. Free
Underground: Marble Arch, Bond Street
Bus: 1, 2, 2B, 13, 26, 30, 59, 74, 74B, 113, 159

Royal Mews
Buckingham Palace Road, SW1W 0QH
Weds & Thurs 14 00 to 16 00
Closed during the Royal Ascot Meeting in June. The horses are sometimes absent on duty
Admission 15p, children 16 & under 5p
see *Victoria BR Station*

Royal National Orthopaedic Hospital
234 Great Portland Street, W1
Underground: Great Portland Street
Bus: 3, 18, 27, 30, 53, 137, 176

Royal Naval College
see *Greenwich*

Royal Observatory
see *Greenwich*

Royal Photographic Society
14 South Audley Street,
W1Y 5DP
see *Wellington Museum*

Royal Society of Arts
8 John Adam Street, WC2
Underground: Strand, Charing Cross
Bus: see *Savoy Chapel*

Rudolf Steiner Hall
33 Park Road, NW1
Underground: Baker Street
Bus: 2, 2B, 13, 26, 59, 74, 74B, 113, 159

RWS Galleries
26 Conduit Street, W1
Underground: Bond Street, Oxford Circus
Bus: 3, 6, 12, 13, 15, 25, 39, 53, 59, 88, 159, 505

St Aidan's Church W3
Underground: East Acton
Bus: 7, 12, 15, 49, 72, 105

St Albans Herts
CATHEDRAL Daily 07 00 to 19 00 (21 00 in summer). Free

CLOCK TOWER Sats & Suns only till 28 May, then daily till mid-Sept, 10 30 to 17 00 (Thurs to 13 00). 5p, children 2½p

ROMAN THEATRE Daily except Christmas Day & Boxing Day 10 00 to dusk. 15p, students 10p, children 16 & under 5p

VERULAMIUM MUSEUM Mons to Sats—in summer 10 00 to 17 30 at other times 10 00 to 16 00
Suns—in summer 14 00 to 17 30 at other times 14 00 to 16 00
Closed Christmas Eve & Day, Boxing Day. Open Good Fri (to 16 00), Easter weekend & Mon (to 17 30), Spring & Late Summer Hol Mons

HYPOCAUST Times as for
Museum (closed Mons to Fris
Nov to Feb)
Museum & Hypocaust 10p
students & children 2½p
(Roman Wall & South East
Gate foundations free)

CITY MUSEUM Hatfield Road
Mons to Sats 10 00 to 17 00
Closed Good Fri, Sat & Mon at
Easter, Spring & Late Summer
Hol Mons, Christmas Day,
Boxing Day. Free

ST MICHAEL'S CHURCH Daily
10 00 to 12 00 (also 14 00 to
18 00 Apr to Sept). Free

Underground: High Barnet
then bus 84

**St Bartholomew the Great
Church** West Smithfield, EC1
see *St Bartholomew's Hospital*

St Bartholomew's Hospital
West Smithfield, EC1
Underground: Barbican,
St Paul's
Bus: 4, 8, 22, 25, 141, 277, 279
501, 502

**St Bride Printing Library &
Museum**
Bride Lane, Fleet Street, EC4
LIBRARY Mons to Fris 09 30 to
17 30
MUSEUM Mons to Fris 10 00 to
17 00
Closed Good Fri, Easter Mon,
Spring & Late Summer Hol
Mons, Christmas Day,
Boxing Day. Free
Underground: Blackfriars
Bus: 4, 6, 9, 11, 15, 17, 45, 63,
141, 168, 168A, 502, 513

St Bride's Church Fleet Street,
EC4
Underground: Blackfriars
Bus: 4, 6, 9, 9A, 11, 15, 502,

513 to *Daily Telegraph* building
in Fleet Street

St Clement Danes Church
Strand, WC2
Underground: Temple
Bus: see *Savoy Chapel*

St Dunstan-in-the-West Church
Fleet Street, EC4
Underground: Temple
Bus: 4, 6, 9, 9A, 11, 15, 171,
502, 513

St Ethelburga's Church
Bishopsgate, EC3
Underground: Liverpool Street
Bus: 6, 8, 8A, 22, 35, 47, 48,
78, 149

St Etheldreda's Church
Ely Place, EC1
see *Ely Place*

St George's Church
Hanover Square, W1
Underground: Oxford Circus
Bus: see *RWS Galleries*

St George's Hospital
Hyde Park Corner, SW1
Underground: Hyde Park Corner
Bus: 2, 2B, 9, 9A, 14, 16, 19,
22, 25, 26, 30, 36, 36A, 36B, 38,
52, 73, 74, 74B, 137, 500

St Helen's Church
Great St Helen's,
Bishopsgate, EC3
see *St Ethelburga's Church*

St James's Church
Piccadilly, W1
Underground: Piccadilly Circus
Bus: 9, 9A, 14, 19, 22, 38, 506

St James's Palace
Pall Mall, SW1
Underground: Green Park
Bus: 9, 9A, 14, 19, 22, 25, 38,
506

St James's Park SW1
Underground: St James's Park, Trafalgar Square, Green Park
Bus: see *Houses of Parliament* and *St James's Palace*

St James's Square SW1
see *Albany*

St John's Church
St John's Square, EC1 and
St John's Gate St John's Lane, Clerkenwell, EC1M 4DA
To view Gate write to the Curator
Underground: Farringdon
Bus: 5, 55, 243, 277, 279

St John's Smith Square, SW1
Underground: Westminster
Bus: 3, 10, 77, 77A, 77B, 88, 149, 159, 168, 168B, 507

St Magnus the Martyr
Lower Thames Street, EC3
Underground: Monument
Bus: 8A, 10, 21, 35, 40, 40A, 43, 44, 47, 48, 133, 501, 513

St Margaret's Church
Parliament Square, SW1
see *Westminster Abbey*

St Martin-in-the-Fields Church
Trafalgar Square, WC2
see *National Gallery*

St Mary-le-Bow Church
see *Guildhall*

St Mary-le-Strand Church
Strand, WC2
Underground: Temple
Bus: see *Savoy Chapel*

St Mary's Hospital
Praed Street, W2
see *Paddington BR Station*

St Nicholas Church
Deptford Green, SE8
Underground: Surrey Docks, then bus 1, 1A, 47, 70, 108B, 188

St Pancras BR Station NW1
see *King's Cross BR Station*

St Paul's Cathedral
St Paul's Churchyard, EC4

CATHEDRAL Daily 07 45 to 19 00 (Oct to Mar to 18 00)—for services only on 25 Jan, Good Fri, Easter Sun, 31 May, Christmas Day

CRYPT, GALLERIES Mons to Sats 10 45 to: Oct to March 15 30; Apr 17 30; May and Sept 18 00; June to Aug 18 30. Closed for services 15 30 to 16 45 daily, 25 Jan, Good Fri, 31 May, Christmas Day Galleries and Library (Library closed Mons) 15p; Crypt 10p
Underground: St Paul's, Mansion House
Bus: 4, 6, 8, 9, 9A, 11, 15, 18, 22, 25, 76, 141, 501, 502, 513

St Paul's Church
Covent Garden, WC2
see *Covent Garden Market*

St Stephen Walbrook
Walbrook, EC4
Underground: Bank, Cannon Street
Bus: 6, 8, 9, 9A, 11, 15, 21, 22, 25, 43, 76, 95, 133, 149, 501, 502, 513

St Thomas's Hospital
Lambeth Palace Road, SE1
Underground: Westminster
Bus: 12, 53, 59, 76, 77C, 109, 149, 155, 168A, 170, 171, 172, 177, 184, 503, 507

Salisbury Hall
London Colney, Herts
HALL and MOSQUITO AIRCRAFT
Suns from Easter to end of Sept
& Thurs from July to Sept
14 00 to 18 00; Easter Mon,
Spring & Late Summer Hol
Mons 10 30 to 12 30 & 14 00 to
17 30. Hall & gardens 20p
children 15 & under 10p
Aircraft 10p, children 5p
Underground: High Barnet
then bus 84

Sandown Park, Esher, Surrey
British Rail: Esher
Bus: 72, 152, 206, 215, 218, 219

**Savoy Chapel (Queen's Chapel
of the Savoy)**
Savoy Hill, Strand, WC2R 0DA
Services Suns 11 15 (not Aug,
Sept), Weds 12 30. Open to public
during middle of day Tues to
Fris except Aug & Boxing Day
Underground: Charing Cross,
Strand, Temple
Bus: 1, 1A, 4, 6, 9, 9A, 11, 13,
15, 68, 77, 77A, 77B 77C, 109,
155, 168, 168B, 170, 171, 172,
176, 184, 188, 196, 239, 502,
505, 513

Science Museum
Exhibition Road,
South Kensington, SW7 2DD
Mons to Sats 10 00 to 18 00
Suns 14 30 to 18 00. Closed
Good Fri, Christmas Eve &
Day, Boxing Day. Open
Easter weekend & Mon,
Spring & Late Summer Hol
Mons. 10p (July & Aug 20p)
children 15 & under & pensioners
5p. Library free
Underground: South Kensington
Bus: 14, 30, 39A, 45, 49, 74,
74B

Scotland Yard Broadway, SW1
see *Queen Anne's Gate*

**Serpentine Gallery
(Arts Council)**
Kensington Gardens, W2
Apr 1 to Oct 15 daily
(including public hols) 11 00 to
dusk. Closed between
exhibitions
Underground: Lancaster Gate
Knightsbridge
Bus: 9, 9A, 52, 73

Seymour Hall
Seymour Place, W1
Underground: Marble Arch,
Marylebone, Edgware Road
(Metropolitan Line)
Bus: 1, 6, 7, 8, 15, 16, 18, 27,
36, 36A, 36B, 176, 616

Shell Centre South Bank, SE1
PUBLIC VIEWING GALLERY
Apr to Oct, Mons to Fris
10 00 to 17 30. Closed Easter
Mon, Spring & Late Summer
Hol Mons. 15p (parties
of 20 or more 10p), children
under 14 5p (unaccompanied
children under 14 not admitted)
Underground: Waterloo
Bus: 1, 4, 68, 70, 76, 149,
168A, 171, 176, 188, 196, 239,
501, 502, 503, 505, 507, 513

Silver Vaults
Chancery Lane, WC2
see *London Silver Vaults*

Sir John Soane's Museum
13 Lincoln's Inn Fields, WC2
Tues to Sats (including Sat at
Easter) 10 00 to 17 00. Closed
Good Fri, throughout Aug,
Boxing Day. Free
Underground: Holborn
Bus: 8, 22, 25, 55, 68, 77,
77A, 77B, 77C, 170, 172, 188,
196, 239, 501

Slade School of Fine Arts
see *University College*

Smithfield Market
Charterhouse Street, EC1
Underground: Farringdon,
Barbican
Bus: 4, 5, 8, 17, 18, 22, 25, 45,
46, 55, 63, 168A, 221, 243, 259,
277, 279

Somerset House Strand, WC2
OFFICE OF POPULATION
CENSUSES AND SURVEYS,
GENERAL REGISTER OFFICE
PUBLIC SEARCH ROOMS
Mons to Fris 09 30 to 16 30,
Sats 09 30 to 12 30. Closed
Good Fri, Sat & Mon at Easter,
Spring & Late Summer Hol
Mons & preceding Sats,
Christmas Day, Boxing Day
Access free

PRINCIPAL REGISTRY OF FAMILY
DIVISION OF HIGH COURT OF
JUSTICE Mons to Fris 10 00
to 16 30. Closed Good Fri,
Easter Mon and Tues, Spring
and Late Summer Hol Mons,
Christmas Day, Boxing Day
Access to Probate index free
see *Australia House*

Sotheby's Auction Rooms
34 New Bond Street, W1
Underground: Bond Street,
Green Park
Bus: 25

South Africa House (Embassy)
Trafalgar Square, WC2N 5DP
Tel: 01-930 4488
OFFICES, LIBRARY AND
READING ROOM
Mons to Fris 09 30 to 12 30 and
14 00 to 16 00. Closed Good Fri,
Easter Mon, Spring & Late
Summer Hol Mons, Christmas
Day, Boxing Day. Free
see *National Gallery*

South Bank Lion
Westminster Bridge, SE1
Underground: Westminster
Bus: 12, 53, 59, 76, 77C, 109,
155, 170, 172, 184, 503

South London Art Gallery
Peckham Road, SE5 8UH
Mons to Sats 10 00 to 18 00
Suns 15 00 to 18 00
Closed between exhibitions
& Good Fri, Easter weekend &
Mon, Spring & Late Summer
Hol Mons, Christmas Eve &
Day, Boxing Day. Free
Underground: Oval then bus 36,
36A, 36B, or Elephant &
Castle then bus 12, 171

Southwark Cathedral
London Bridge, SE1
Underground: London Bridge
Bus: 8A, 10, 18, 21, 35, 40,
40A, 43, 44, 47, 48, 70, 133,
501, 513

Spitalfields Market
Commercial Street, E1
Daily except Suns
Underground: Liverpool Street
Bus: 5, 6, 8, 8A, 22, 35, 47, 48,
67, 78, 97, 149

Staple Inn Holborn, WC2
Underground: Chancery Lane
Bus: 8, 17, 18, 22, 25, 45, 46,
171, 243. 259, 501

Stock Exchange
Old Broad Street, EC2
Visitors' Gallery and Cinema:
Mons to Fris 10 00 to 15 15.
Closed Good Fri, Easter Mon,
Spring & Late Summer Hol
Mons, Christmas Eve & Day,
Boxing Day. Free
see *Bank of England*

Strand WC2
Underground: Strand,
Trafalgar Square

Bus: 1, 1A, 6, 9, 9A, 11, 13, 15, 77, 77A, 77B, 77C, 170, 176, 505

Strand-on-the-Green
Chiswick, W4
Underground: Gunnersbury
then bus 27, 117, 267
Bus: 15, 65

Strawberry Hill
St Mary's College of
Education, Waldegrave Road,
Twickenham, Middlesex
To view write to the Principal
Underground: Richmond then
bus 27, 270

**Streatham (Silver Blades)
Ice Rink**
Streatham High Road, SW16
Underground: Brixton then
bus 50, 57A, 59, 109, 133, 159
Bus: 49, 95, 115, 115A, 118,
130, 181, 249

Swakeleys House The Avenue,
Ickenham, Middlesex
Tues, Wed, Thurs 09 00 to 17 00,
Sats & Suns 11 00 to 17 00.
Closed Good Fri, Easter Mon,
Spring & Late Summer Hol
Mons, Christmas Eve & Day,
Boxing Day. Open Sat & Sun at
Easter. Free
Underground: Ickenham
Bus: 223, 273

Swimming
CAMDEN OASIS SWIMMING POOL
Endell Street, WC2
Underground: Tottenham Court
Road, Covent Garden
Bus: 1, 14, 24, 29, 73, 176
(all southbound);
7, 8, 19, 22, 25, 38 (all
westbound)

HAMPSTEAD POND
South End Green, NW3
Underground: Belsize Park
then bus 187
Bus: 24, 46, 268, C11

HIGHGATE BATHING POOL
Parliament Hill, N6
(Men only)
Underground: Camden Town
then bus 214
Bus: C11

HYDE PARK LIDO Hyde Park, W2
Underground: Hyde Park
Bus: 2, 2B, 6, 7, 8, 9, 9A, 12,
14, 15, 16, 19, 22, 25, 26, 30,
36, 36A, 36B, 38, 52, 73, 74,
74B, 88, 137, 500, 616

KENWOOD BATHING POND
(Ladies only)
Underground: Archway or
Golders Green then bus 210

MARSHALL STREET BATHS W1
Underground: Oxford Circus,
Piccadilly Circus
Bus: 3, 6, 12, 13, 15, 39, 53, 59
88, 159, 505

PARLIAMENT HILL LIDO NW5
Underground: Camden Town
then bus 214

RICKMANSWORTH AQUADROME
Rickmansworth, Herts
Underground: Rickmansworth

RUISLIP LIDO Ruislip, Middlesex
Underground: Ruislip then
bus 114

SWISS COTTAGE BATHS
Winchester Road, NW3
Underground: Swiss Cottage
Bus: 2, 2B, 13, 26, 31, 113, 187,
268, C11

Syon House
Brentford. Middlesex
19 April to 28 July Mons to
Fris (including Good Fri) &
Sat & Sun at Easter 13 00 to
17 00 (11 00 to 17 00 Easter
Mon & Spring Hol Mon).
29 July to 7 Oct Suns to Thurs
13 00 to 17 00 (11 00 to 17 00
Late Summer Hol Mon).
Last ticket 45 mins before

closing time 30p, children 16 & under 10p, students & pensioners 20p
For Brent Lea Gate, Brentford
Underground: Hammersmith then bus 267
Bus: 117
For Isleworth Gate
Bus: 37

Tate Gallery
Millbank, SW1P 4RG
Mons to Sats 10 00 to 18 00
Suns 14 00 to 18 00. Closed Good Fri, Christmas Eve & Day, Boxing Day
Open Easter weekend & Mon, Spring & Late Summer Hol Mons. Admission charges under consideration
Underground: Pimlico
Bus: 77B, 88

Television Centre (BBC)
Wood Lane, W12
see *White City Stadium*

Temple EC4
INNER TEMPLE HALL
Usually open (not on public hols) Mons to Fris
10 00 to 11 30 & 14 30 to 16 00
during legal terms

MIDDLE TEMPLE HALL
Middle Temple Lane
Sats 10 00 to 16 00 Usually also Mons to Fris 10 00 to 12 00 & 15 00 to 16 30. Closed Easter Mon, Spring & Late Summer Hol Mons, Christmas Day, Boxing Day, & when in use for Inn activities

TEMPLE CHURCH 10 00 to 17 00 (to 16 30 in winter). Good Fri 14 00 to 16 00, Sat at Easter 10 00 to 16 30, Easter Sun 14 00 to 16 00, Easter Mon & Spring Hol Mon 10 00 to 16 30
Usual hours Late Summer Hol

Mon & Christmas Eve. Closed Christmas Day except for services, & Boxing Day. Free
Underground: Temple
Bus: 4, 6, 9, 9A, 11, 15, 171, 502, 513

Temple Bar Theobald's Park, Cheshunt, Herts
Bus: 205, 205A, 242, 279

Temple of Mithras
Queen Victoria Street, at Cannon Street, EC4
Underground: Bank, Mansion House
Bus: see *Bank of England*

Thamesmead SE2 & SE28
British Rail: Abbey Wood
Bus: 177, 180, 180A, 229

Theatres
ADELPHI Strand, WC2
see *Charing Cross BR Station*

ALBERY'S St Martin's Lane, WC2
see *Theatres—Duke of York's*

ALDWYCH, Aldwych, WC2
Underground: Covent Garden, Holborn, Temple
Bus: 1, 1A, 4, 6, 9, 9A, 11, 13, 15, 55, 68, 77, 77A, 77B, 77C, 170, 171, 172, 176, 188, 196, 239, 502, 505, 513

AMBASSADORS West Street, Shaftesbury Avenue, WC2
Underground: Leicester Square
Bus: 1, 14, 19, 22, 24, 29, 38, 176

APOLLO
Shaftesbury Avenue, WC2
Underground: Piccadilly Circus
Bus: 14, 19, 22, 38

BANKSIDE GLOBE SUMMER THEATRE Emerson Street, SE1
Underground: Mansion House,

Cannon Street, London Bridge
Bus: 18, 44, 70, 95, 149, 176A

CAMBRIDGE Earlham Street,
Cambridge Circus, WC2
Underground: Covent Garden,
Leicester Square
Bus: 1, 14, 19, 22, 24, 29, 38,
176

COLISEUM (Sadler's Wells
Opera Company) St Martin's
Lane, WC2
see *Theatres—Duke of York's*

COMEDY Panton Street, SW1
Underground: Piccadilly Circus
Bus: 3, 6, 9, 9A, 12, 13, 14, 15,
19, 22, 38, 39, 53, 59, 159, 505,
506

COVENT GARDEN
see *Theatres—Royal Opera
House*

CRITERION Piccadilly Circus, W1
see *Theatres—Comedy*

DRURY LANE THEATRE ROYAL
WC2
see *Theatres—Aldwych*

DUCHESS Catherine Street, WC2
see *Theatres—Aldwych*

DUKE OF YORK'S
St Martin's Lane, WC2
Underground: Leicester Square
Bus: 1, 24, 29, 176

FORTUNE Russell Street, WC2
see *Theatres—Aldwych*

GARRICK
Charing Cross Road, WC2
see *Theatres—Duke of York's*

GLOBE Shaftesbury Avenue, W1
see *Theatres—Apollo*

GREENWICH THEATRE
Crooms Hill, SE10
Underground: Surrey Docks
then bus 1A, 70, 108B, 188
British Rail: Greenwich
Bus: 177, 180, 180A, 185

HAYMARKET THEATRE ROYAL
Haymarket, SW1
see *Theatres—Comedy*

HER MAJESTY'S
Haymarket, SW1
see *Theatres—Comedy*

JEANNETTA COCHRANE
Southampton Row, WC2
Underground: Holborn
Bus: 5, 7, 8, 19, 22, 25, 38,
55, 68, 77, 77A, 77C, 170, 172,
188, 196, 239, 501

LYRIC Shaftesbury Avenue, W1
see *Theatres—Apollo*

MAYFAIR Stratton Street, W1
Underground: Green Park
Bus: 9, 9A, 14, 19, 22, 25, 38,
506

MERMAID Puddle Dock, EC4
Underground: Blackfriars
Bus: 17, 45, 63, 76, 109, 141,
155, 168, 168A, 168B, 184

NEW LONDON Parker Street,
Drury Lane, WC2
see *Freemasons' Hall*

OLD VIC Waterloo Road, SE1
YOUNG VIC The Cut, SE1
Underground: Waterloo
Bus: 1, 1A, 4, 68, 70, 76, 176,
188, 196, 239, 501, 502, 505,
513

OPEN AIR THEATRE Inner Circle,
Regent's Park, NW1
Underground: Baker Street,
Regent's Park
Bus: 1, 2, 2B, 13, 18, 26, 27, 30,
59, 74, 74B, 113, 159, 176

PALACE Cambridge Circus, W1
Underground: Leicester Square,
Tottenham Court Road
Bus: see *Theatres—Ambassadors*

PALLADIUM Argyll Street, W1
Underground: Oxford Circus
Bus: 1, 3, 6, 7, 8, 12, 13, 15, 25,
39, 53, 59, 73, 88, 113, 137,
159, 500, 505, 616

PHOENIX
Charing Cross Road, WC2
Underground: Tottenham
Court Road
Bus: 1, 7, 8, 14, 19, 22, 24, 25,
29, 38, 73, 176

PICCADILLY **Denman Street,**
Piccadilly Circus, W1
see *Theatres—Comedy*

THE PLACE **Duke's Road, WC1**
Underground: Euston, Euston
Square
Bus: 14, 18, 30, 68, 73, 77, 77A,
77B, 77C, 170, 188, 196, 239

PRINCE OF WALES
Coventry Street, W1
see *Theatres—Comedy*

QUEEN'S
Shaftesbury Avenue, W1
see *Theatres—Comedy*

ROUND HOUSE
see main entry

ROYAL COURT
Sloane Square, SW1
Underground: Sloane Square
Bus: 11, 19, 22, 137

ROYAL OPERA HOUSE
Covent Garden, WC2
Underground: Covent Garden,
Leicester Square
Bus: 1, 6, 9, 9A, 11, 13, 15, 77,
77A, 77B, 77C, 170, 176, 505

ROYALTY **Kingsway, WC2**
Underground: Holborn
Bus: 55, 68, 77, 77A, 77B, 77C,
170, 172, 188, 196, 239, 501

SADLER'S WELLS
Rosebery Avenue, EC1
Underground: Angel
Bus: 19, 38, 171, 172, 279

ST MARTIN'S **West Street,**
Cambridge Circus, WC2
see *Theatres—Ambassadors*

SAVOY **Strand, WC2**
Underground: Strand,
Covent Garden. Temple
Bus: see *Theatres—Aldwych*

SHAFTESBURY
Shaftesbury Avenue, WC2
Underground: Holborn,
Covent Garden
Bus: 1, 7, 8, 14, 19, 22, 24,
25, 29, 38, 73, 176

SHAW
100 Euston Road, NW1 2AJ
Young people (under 21) &
students & pensioners half-price
all performances
see *King's Cross BR Station*

STRAND **Aldwych, WC2**
see *Theatres—Aldwych*

THEATRE ROYAL **Stratford, E15**
Underground: Stratford
Bus: 10, 25, 69, 86, 169A, 238,
241, 262, S1, S3

VAUDEVILLE **Strand, WC2**
see *Charing Cross BR Station*

VICTORIA PALACE
Victoria Street, SW1
see *Victoria BR Station*

WESTMINSTER
Palace Street, SW1
see *Victoria BR Station*

WHITEHALL
Trafalgar Square, SW1
Underground: Trafalgar Square,
Strand, Charing Cross
Bus: 1, 1A, 3, 6, 9, 9A, 11, 12,
13, 15, 24, 29, 39, 53, 59, 76,
77, 77A, 77B, 77C, 88, 159,
168, 168B, 170, 176, 505

WIMBLEDON **Broadway, SW19**
Underground: Wimbledon
Bus: 57, 77A, 77C, 93, 131,
155, 200, 293

WYNDHAM'S
Charing Cross Road, WC2
see *Theatres—Duke of York's*

Tower of London
Tower Hill, EC3
Mar to Oct Mons to Sats
09 30 to 17 00, Suns 14 00 to
17 00; Nov to Feb Mons to

47

Sats only 09 30 to 16 00. Closed
Good Fri, Christmas Eve &
Day, Boxing Day. Open
Easter weekend & Mon,
Spring & Late Summer Hol
Mons. 40p (winter 20p),
pensioners & children 5p
(under-fives free)
Unaccompanied children not
admitted

JEWEL HOUSE 15p (Summer),
10p (Winter), children &
pensioners 5p

ROYAL FUSILIERS MUSEUM 2½p
Underground: Tower Hill
Bus: 9A, 42, 78

Tower Pier EC3
see *Tower of London*

Trafalgar Square WC2
see *National Gallery*

TUC Headquarters
see *Congress House*

Madame Tussaud's
Marylebone Road, NW1 5LR
Daily except Christmas Day
Apr to Sept daily (including
Easter weekend & Mon,
Spring & Late Summer Hol
Mons) 10 00 to 18 30; Oct to
Mar Mons to Fris 10 00 to 17 30
(Good Fri to 18 30, Christmas
Eve to 17 00), Sats & Suns &
Boxing Day 10 00 to 18 30
55p (70p from 1 April), children
14 & under & pensioners
30p (35p from 1 April)
Royal ticket including
Planetarium 75p (85p from
1 April), children & pensioners
35p (40p from 1 April)
see also *Planetarium*
Underground: Baker Street
Bus: 1, 2, 2B, 13, 18, 26, 27, 30,
59, 74, 74B, 113, 159, 176

Tyburn Marble Arch, W1
see *Marble Arch*

Unilever House
Victoria Embankment, EC4
Underground: Blackfriars
Bus: 17, 45, 63, 76, 109, 141,
155, 168, 168A, 168B, 184

**University College and
Hospital**
Gower Street, WC1E 6BT
Underground: Euston Square,
Warren Street
Bus: 14, 18, 24, 29, 30, 73, 134,
176, 253

University of London
Senate House, Malet Street
and Russell Square, WC1
Underground: Goodge Street,
Russell Square
Bus: 14, 24, 29, 73, 176 to
Gower Street; 68, 77, 77A, 77C,
170, 188, 196, 239 to Russell
Square

Verulamium—see *St Albans*

Vickers Building Millbank, SW1
Underground: Vauxhall or
Westminster then bus 77B, 88;
Victoria then bus 10, 149, 507

Victoria and Albert Museum
Cromwell Road.
South Kensington, SW7 2RL
Mons to Sats 10 00 to 18 00
Suns 14 30 to 18 00. Closed
Good Fri, Christmas Eve & Day,
Boxing Day. Open Easter
weekend & Mon. Spring &
Late Summer Hol Mons
Admission charges
under consideration
see *Science Museum*

Victoria Coach Station
Buckingham Palace Road, SW1
Underground: Victoria
Bus: 11, 39

Victoria BR Station SW1
Underground: Victoria
Bus: 2, 2B, 10A, 11, 16, 24, 25,
26, 29, 36, 36A, 36B, 38, 39, 52,
149, 181, 185, 500, 503, 506, 507

Wallace Collection
Hertford House,
Manchester Square, W1M 6BN
Mons to Sats 1000 to 1700
Suns 1400 to 1700
Closed Good Fri, Christmas
Eve & Day. Open Easter
weekend & Mon, Spring &
Late Summer Hol Mons,
Boxing Day. Admission charges
under consideration
Underground: Bond Street
Bus: 1, 2, 2B, 13, 26, 30, 59,
74, 74B, 113, 159 to Portman
Square; 6, 7, 8, 12, 15, 73, 88,
137, 500, 505, 616 to Selfridge's

Waltham Abbey
Waltham Holy Cross, Essex
Bus: 205, 205A, 217, 217A, 242

**Waltham Cross
(Queen Eleanor's Cross)**
High Street,
Waltham Cross, Herts
Bus: 205, 205A, 217, 217A,
242, 279

Walthamstow Stadium
Chingford Road, E4
Underground: Walthamstow
Central then bus 69, 256, 262,
276, W21
Bus: 34, 58, 144 to Crooked
Billet then short walk

Waterloo Place
Regent Street, SW1
Underground: Trafalgar Square,
Piccadilly Circus
Bus: see *Piccadilly Circus*

Waterloo BR Station SE1
Underground: Waterloo
Bus: 1, 1A, 4, 68, 70, 76, 149,
168A, 171, 176, 188, 196, 239,
501, 502, 503, 505, 507, 513

Waterlow Park Highgate, N6
Underground: Archway
Bus: 210, 271, C11 (then
short walk)

**Wellcome Institute of the
History of Medicine**
183 Euston Road, NW1
MUSEUM AND LIBRARY
Mons to Sats 1000 to 1700
Closed Good Fri, Sat & Mon
at Easter, Spring & Late
Summer Hol Mons &
preceding Sats, Christmas Day,
Boxing Day. Free
see *University College and
Hospital*

Well Hall
Well Hall Road, Eltham, SE9
TUDOR BARN Apr to Sept
daily except Sats 1100 to 2000
Oct to Mar daily except
Sats 1030 (Suns 1130) to dusk
Closed Christmas Eve & Day,
Boxing Day. Open Good Fri,
Easter Sun & Mon, Spring &
Late Summer Hol Mons. Free
British Rail: Eltham
(Well Hall)
Bus: 21, 21A, 61, 89, 108, 126,
132, 161, 161A, 227, 228, B1

Wellington Barracks
Birdcage Walk, SW1
Underground: St James's Park
Bus: 10, 11, 24, 29, 39, 149,
503, 507
see also *Guards Museum*

Wellington Museum
Apsley House,
Hyde Park Corner, W1
Mons to Sats 1000 to 1800
Suns 1430 to 1800. Closed
Good Fri, Christmas Eve &
Day, Boxing Day. Open Sat,
Sun & Mon at Easter, Spring &
Late Summer Hol Mons
10p (July & Aug 20p)
children 16 & under 5p
school parties free

Underground: Hyde Park Corner
Bus: 2, 2B, 9, 9A, 14, 16, 19,
22, 25, 26, 30, 36, 36A, 36B, 38,
52, 73, 74, 74B, 137, 500

**Wembley Stadium and
Empire Pool**
Empire Way,
Wembley, Middlesex
Underground: Wembley Park,
Wembley Central
Bus: 8, 18, 83, 92, 182, 297

Wesley's Chapel and House
City Road, EC1Y 1AU
CHAPEL closed until further
notice
HOUSE Mons, Weds to Sats
10 00 to 13 00 and 14 00 to
16 00 (not Fris)
Closed Good Fri, Easter Mon,
Spring & Late Summer Hol
Mons, Christmas Day,
Boxing Day. Open Sat
at Easter. 10p
Underground: Old Street
Bus: 5, 43, 55, 76, 104, 141,
214, 243, 271

West Ham Stadium
Custom House, E16
Underground: Plaistow then
bus 262
Bus: 175

West London Air Terminal
see *Air Terminals*

Westminster Abbey
Broad Sanctuary, SW1
Daily 08 00 to 18 00
(Weds to 20 00)
CHAPELS AND AMBULATORY
Mons to Thurs 10 00 to 16 00,
Fris 10 00 to 15 45, Sats 10 00
to 14 00 & 15 45 to 17 00
Open for services only
Good Fri, Christmas Day,
Boxing Day
15p, children 5p (Weds 18 00 to
20 00 free)

NORMAN UNDERCROFT
(Abbey Treasures Exhibition)
Mons to Sats 09 30 to 17 00.
Closed Good Fri,
Christmas Day, Boxing Day
Open Sat & Mon at Easter,
Spring & Late Summer Hol
Mons, Christmas Eve. 10p,
children 5p.
Underground: Westminster,
St James's Park
Bus: 3, 11, 12, 24, 29, 39, 53,
59, 76, 77, 77A, 77B, 77C, 88,
109, 155, 159, 168, 168B, 170,
172, 184, 503

Westminster Cathedral
Ashley Place, SW1
Usually daily 06 00 to 21 00
Good Fri & Sat at Easter
09 00 to 21 00, Easter Sun
05 30 to 21 00, Easter Mon &
Spring & Late Summer Hol
Mons 07 00 to 21 00, Christmas
Eve 06 00 to 21 00, Christmas
Day 05 30 to 21 00, Boxing
Day 06 30 to 16 30 (Sat at
Easter & Christmas Eve
Midnight Mass from 22 30)
Free
TOWER 10p, children 5p
see *Victoria BR Station*

**Westminster Central
Reference Library**
St Martin's Street,
Leicester Square, W1
see *Cinemas—Odeon, Leicester
Square*

Westminster Hall
see *Houses of Parliament*

Westminster Hospital
Horseferry Road, SW1
Underground: Westminster,
St James's Park
Bus: 3, 10, 77, 77A, 77B, 88,
149, 159, 168, 168B, 507

Westminster Pier
Victoria Embankment, SW1
River trips, tel: 01-930 1661

Underground: Westminster
Bus: see *Westminster Abbey*

Westminster School
Dean's Yard, SW1
see *Westminster Abbey*

Whitechapel Art Gallery
High Street, E1
Telephone for details of
exhibitions, hours, charges—
01-247 1492
Underground: Aldgate East
Bus: 5, 10, 15, 23, 25, 40, 40A,
67, 253

White City Stadium
Wood Lane, W12
Underground: White City
Bus: 72, 105, 220

Whitehall SW1
Underground: Westminster,
Strand, Charing Cross,
Trafalgar Square
Bus: 3, 11, 12, 24, 29, 39, 53,
59, 76, 77, 77A, 77B, 77C, 88,
159, 168, 168B, 170

White Lodge
Richmond Park, Surrey
House & Grounds may be
visited by arrangement with
the Bursar, Royal Ballet School,
155 Talgarth Road, W14
Underground: Putney Bridge
then bus 85
Bus: 72

Wigmore Hall
36 Wigmore Street, W1
Underground: Bond Street
Oxford Circus
Bus: 159

**William Morris Gallery and
Brangwyn Gift**
Lloyd Park, Forest Road,
Walthamstow, E17 4PP
Mons to Sats 10 00 to 13 00 and
14 00 to 17 00 (until 20 00 on
Tues and Thurs, April to
Sept only). First Sun in the

month (not Easter Sun)
10 00 to 12 00 & 14 00 to 17 00
Closed Good Fri, Easter
weekend & Mon, Spring &
Late Summer Hol Mons,
Christmas Day, Boxing Day
Free
Underground: Walthamstow
Central
Bus: 34, 55, 69, 123, 262, 275,
276, W21

**Wimbledon Common and
Putney Heath SW19**
Underground: Putney Bridge
then bus 74, 85, 85A, 93;
Wimbledon then bus 93
Bus: 28, 72, 168, 168B

**Wimbledon Lawn Tennis
Ground** Church Road, SW19
Underground: Southfields,
Wimbledon, then special coach
service during the Wimbledon
championships

Wimbledon Stadium
Plough Lane, SW17
Underground: Wimbledon or
Tooting Broadway then
Express Bus
Bus: 44, 77, 77A, 77B, 77C,
189, 220, or 200 to Haydons
Road station then short walk

Woolwich Free Ferry
Bus: 40A, 51, 51A, 53, 54, 69,
75, 96, 99, 101, 122, 122A, 124,
161, 161A, 177, 180, 180A, 192,
229

York House Riverside,
Twickenham, Middlesex
HOUSE View by arrangement with
London Borough of Richmond
upon Thames. Free
GROUNDS Daily dawn to dusk,
free
Underground: Richmond then
bus 27, 90, 90B, 202, 270
Bus: 33, 73, 110, 267, 281

Zoo—see *London Zoo*

WEEKEND, HOLIDAY & OTHER SPECIAL ARRANGEMENTS

Certain Underground stations are **closed at weekends.**

Closed on Saturdays and Sundays

Aldwych	Mornington Crescent
Barbican	Roding Valley
Cannon Street	Shoreditch
Essex Road	West Brompton
Fairlop	

Closed on Sundays

Blake Hall	Ravenscourt Park
Chancery Lane	Shadwell
Covent Garden	Temple

Aldwych and Shoreditch are open on Mondays to Fridays at **peak hours only.**

Certain stations are also **closed on public holidays.**

The times at which stations are open may also vary.

If you are travelling at these holiday times, look for the posters detailing special arrangements throughout the Underground which are displayed at all Underground stations before each holiday.

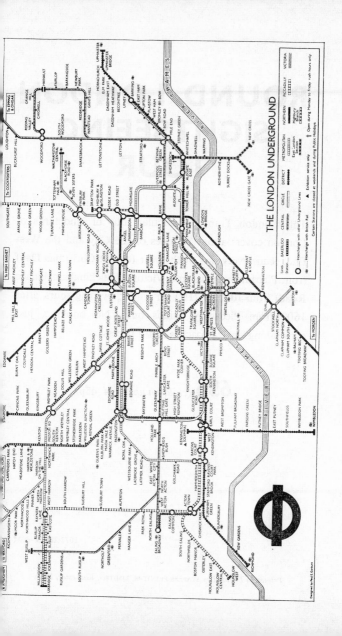

THE LONDON UNDERGROUND

Designed by Paul E Garbutt

Lines : BAKERLOO   CENTRAL   CIRCLE   DISTRICT   METROPOLITAN   NORTHERN   PICCADILLY   VICTORIA

Station   Interchange with other Underground Lines   Interchange with British Rail   Exhibition service only

Certain Stations are closed at weekends and during Public Holidays

East London Section

▲ Open during Monday to Friday rush hours only   Exhibition Stations are closed at weekends and during Public Holidays

ROUND LONDON SIGHTSEEING TOUR

This London Transport circular tour of landmarks of London covers about 20 miles of the City and the West End. Runs every day of the year (except Christmas Day) from Piccadilly Circus and Victoria (Buckingham Palace Road) from 1000 to 2100. In winter, evening tours after 1600 from Piccadilly Circus only. No booking, just come along—extra coaches run if necessary.

65p *(children under 14 45p)*

1072/206RP/50M

Printed in England by STAPLES PRINTERS, LIMITED, *Rochester, Kent.*

Go-as-you-please Tourist Tickets

These give you unlimited* travel on Red Buses and the Underground. Use them for *all* your travel in and around London. They save you time and trouble with change and ticket-buying. You can use them as often as you like on the Underground and buses, and they save you having to buy a ticket for each journey. Go-as-you-please Tourist Tickets really do mean trouble-free travel during your stay in London. Buy Go-as-you-please Tourist Tickets at London Transport Travel Enquiries Offices, at the Tourist Ticket Office, St. James's Park Station, or at certain Underground stations.

Go-as-you-please Tourist Ticket Prices:

FOR 7 CONSECUTIVE DAYS' TRAVEL on all London Transport buses and the Underground as far out as Northwood, Hatch End and Debden, and for ONE trip on the Round London Sightseeing Tour:

£3.80 (child £1.50)

FOR 4 CONSECUTIVE DAYS' TRAVEL as above: £2.90 (child £1.30)

* These tickets are not available on the Underground beyond Northwood, Debden or Harrow & Wealdstone, or on Conducted Coach Tours or other special services. Prices subject to variation.

London Bus
BARGAIN
TICKETS

Red Bus Rovers

take you anywhere, any day, on all normal services of London's red buses (except on sightseeing and coach tours and other special services) after 09 30 on Mondays to Fridays and at any time on Saturdays and Sundays

50p (child 25p)

Red Bus Season Tickets

If you use buses regularly, these tickets are for you. Unlimited travel on London's red bus network (except on the special services mentioned above) and there's no peak hour restriction on their use

Monthly £6

Annual Red Bus Season Tickets are also available on application to the Fares and Charges Office, London Transport, 55 Broadway, London SW1.

Buy Red Bus Rovers or Red Bus Seasons (monthly) at any London Transport Travel Enquiry Office—at Piccadilly Circus, Oxford Circus, King's Cross, Euston, Victoria and St. James's Park Underground Stations—at London Transport garages, at certain Underground stations or from agents of National Travel (N.B.C.) Ltd. in the London area.